THE FORTS OF INDIA

PREVIOUS BOOKS
THE PALACES OF INDIA
VIRGINIA FASS AND
THE MAHARAJA OF BARODA

VIRGINIA FASS

THE FORTS OF INDIA

FOREWORD BY
THE MAHARAJA OF JAIPUR

TEXT BY RITA AND VIJAY SHARMA
AND CHRISTOPHER TADGELL

COLLINS
8 Grafton Street, London W1
in association with
OBEROI HOTELS INTERNATIONAL
1986

William Collins Sons and Co Ltd
London · Glasgow · Sydney · Auckland
Toronto · Johannesburg

British Library Cataloguing in Publication Data

The Forts of India
  I. Fortification—India
  I. Fass, Virginia   II. Sharma, Rita
  945.4   UG432.I

  ISBN 0 00 217590 8

First published 1986

Designed by Ronald Clark
Plans by Christopher Tadgell,
John Quinn and Edward Cuschieri
Typeset in Monophoto Apollo by
Ace Filmsetting Ltd, Frome, Somerset
Colour and Monochrome origination by
Gilchrist Bros, Leeds
Made and Printed in Great Britain by
William Collins Sons and Co Ltd, Glasgow

To my husband Tikki
'With a tear and a smile'.

Jutta and Arjun Oberoi

CONTENTS

FOREWORD

In the constant struggle for power, forts and fortified settlements were a potent symbol of authority. Thus, in ancient India as elsewhere, forts were the measure of a monarch's strength.

There are many references to forts and fortifications in ancient and mediaeval literature dating from Vedic times. The *Rigveda Samhita* mentions tribes living in fortifications called *pur*, meaning earthworks strengthened by stone walls. The *Aiteraya Brahmana* refers to the three *agnis*, or fires, as three forts which prevent the *asuras* from disturbing the sacrifice. The *Ramayana* and the *Mahabharata* also contain accounts of forts, and the *Puranas* state that the rampart and ditch are vital elements in the fortifications of a castle. Kautilya's *Arthshastra* gives a vivid account of the fortified city of Pataliputra, capital of the great Maurya Empire, third century BC, which is supported by subsequent excavations in the modern city of Patna.

Durg is the Indian term for fort, and means difficult to trespass, signifying the importance of a strategic site, a strong wall and a moat to make it an impregnable bastion. There were six types of forts: the *dhanva durg* or desert fort; the *mahi durg* or mud fort; the *jala durg* or water fort; the *giri durg* or hill fort; the *vriksha* or *vana durg*, or forest fort; and the *nara durg* or fort protected by men. Of these the *giri durg* was considered the best, though the *Mahabharata* claims that the *nara durg* was the strongest because a collection of able and trusted men is a king's greatest asset.

One of the most crucial requirements of a fort was a regular supply of water to ensure self-sufficiency during a siege, which could last for months. The planner in the past gave great thought to the availability of this life-saving element by laying down guidelines on storage and efficient reservoir systems. The source of water was a closely guarded secret to prevent the unscrupulous enemy from poisoning it. Varahamir states in his *Brihat Samhita* that arteries of flowing water lie at various depths beneath the surface of the earth, and these can be located by an understanding of topography and environment. However, where natural resources of water were scarce, as in the case of forts in the Rajasthan desert, a common method of storing rainwater in tanks was devised. A number of texts were written on *Vastuvidya* or the art of architecture, which cover the building of *durgs*. These include the *Narada Shilpashastra, Maurya, Aparajita Prichha, Vasturajaballabha Vastumandane, Vastumanjari* and *Mayamata*.

The discovery of gunpowder was the great invention of mediaeval times, leading to the added power of artillery. But the use of cannons to breach impregnable ramparts did not in any way reduce the strength of the fort. Instead, forts equipped themselves with *kharkhna*, run by blacksmiths who cast cannons and manufactured new weapons so that both sides were evenly balanced.

But the forts were not simply inanimate buildings serving a military purpose; they housed some of the most magnificent palaces ever built. They were alive and echoing to the sounds and cymbals of some of the great dynasties, witness to regicides and bloody succession battles, and carrying within their bastions harems and glitter unsurpassed. Thus, when writing the history of any era, of any empire, it is the forts of that period which dominate the rise and fall of fortunes.

These impressive features of our past are the subject of this fascinating book by Virginia Fass, the well known photographer, whose earlier book on Indian Palaces has been greatly appreciated. She has brought to light little known facts about the Rajput and Maratha forts which are scattered throughout modern Rajasthan, Uttar Pradesh and Maharashtra. This is a valuable contribution to the history of warfare in ancient and mediaeval India.

MAHARAJA OF JAIPUR

CITY PALACE JAIPUR

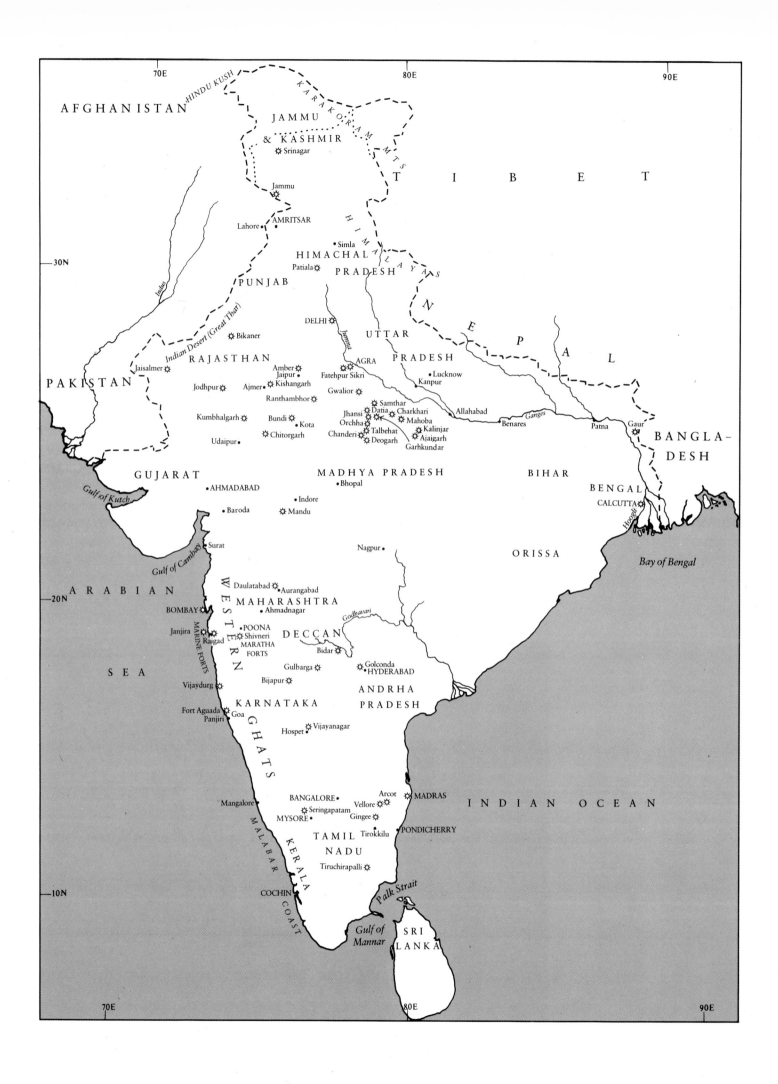

INTRODUCTION

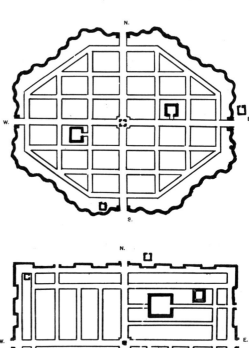

The entire land of Hindusthan is studded with imposing fortresses, many more than those selected in this book. Kings ruled from them and lesser chiefs built them to demonstrate their strength. Their origins are usually lost in antiquity, but most of India's forts were transformed after the Muslim invasion of the 12th century, and although some retain early work, India's Hindu legacy in building is revealed primarily in its great literature.

The earliest treatises (*shastras*) on Indian architecture were compiled from material found in ancient India's great corpus of religious, political and scientific literature. Foremost among these are the commentaries on religious practice related to the Vedic sacred canon, old when the Aryan tribes from central Asia invaded India in the second millenium BC. More specific information on settlement and defence is given in the great epic poems, the *Ramayana* and *Mahabharata*, which emerged in the first millenium BC from the bardic legends about the Aryan conquest. Much has been gleaned, too, from the later Jataka collection of folklore about the life of Buddha, especially as this was illustrated in great reliefs like those of Sanchi.

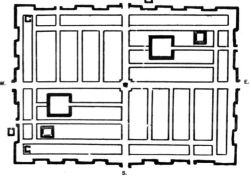

Foremost among the professional theorists was Kautilya. Writing for Chandragupta Maurya, the first historical Emperor of India, in the last quarter of the 4th century BC, his classification of forts is based on preferred types of site. Best were those perched on precipitous rocky outcrops with a town at their base, or isolated by tracts of wilderness or water. Often, however, strategy over-ruled tactics, and a fort had to be founded on the open plain; then water was introduced and the land beyond laid waste to form a moat and a *maidan*, a field open to the fire of the defenders. Kautilya, acknowledging his master's imperial achievements, goes further and classifies metropolitan, provincial and border forts. Beyond their natural advantages, or artificial devices, the strength of all six types depended upon ramparts and the materials used in them – mud, stone, timber etc. The *nara durg* reflects the Aryan identity of fort and town: the camp of tribal warriors which developed, with agriculture, into a place of refuge for peasants and their animals, defended by earthworks and timber palisade. While a variety of shapes were used, according to the nature of the site – a half-moon, for instance, in the bend of a river – rectangles were preferred.

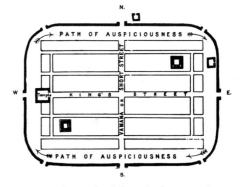

Ancient Indian ideal fortified town plans.

The *shastra* rules for consecrating and laying out the site of a camp, fort, village or town are similar, and apply also to the sacred Vedic sacrificial enclosure. Kautilya's planning starts with two major axial roads aligned with the four cardinal points. These, with parallel subsidiary routes, divided the town into wards graded to accommodate the various castes. The gods were installed at the central crossing, the king to its north. Within the ramparts was a ring road corresponding to the path around a sacred site.

11

Ancient town with Elephant Gate (Sanchi, Great Stupa gatepost relief).

The ramparts themselves were formed of mud dug from ditches. Kautilya calls for three ditches outside the ramparts, spiked and filled variously with sand, mud, and constantly flowing water, diverted from the river and preferably alive with crocodiles. The ramparts should be planted with poisonous bushes and crowned by several ring walls of brick, graded in height and twice as high as they were broad. These had roofed walks wide enough to accommodate patrols in both directions, and square towers. Gates, between twin towers and large enough for elephants, opened the main axes of the town. Each was preceded by a drawbridge spanning the moat, and within them assailants were to be thwarted by a wide range of obstacles, including tortuous deflection of the path, concealed pits, and ditches filled with thorns and sand or water, knee breakers etc.

Kautilya warns that the master of a fort must be wary of the silting-up of ditches, delapidation of the walls and towers, depletion of the arsenal, obsolete weapons and, perhaps most importantly, of corruption and intrigue. An enemy would try to dislodge him not by force but by stratagem. He might try to deceive him into thinking his intentions were honourable, or overawe him by sending him accounts of his prowess and close association with several deities; he might send jugglers and magicians to divert and charm his subjects; his merchants might be wooed with tales of greater profits to be won elsewhere. He had advice for besieging, too: destroy crops and contaminate water only if on the defensive. Take the offensive when there was disease or dissention in the fort or its equipment was faulty. Then the moats should be filled, walls undermined, gates forced with elephants. Fire should be used only as last resort – even Kautilya thought it immoral – through incendiary missiles and by binding brands to the tails of birds.

The early reliefs indicate some crenellation, embrasures for marksmen and battering (sloping of walls). Even the earliest texts mention the former but the much later 'Indian Vetruvius', the elusive Manasara, is unusual in referring to battering. The projection of the gate towers' top storeys may have provided for the dropping of stones and boiling oil onto assailants, though there is little evidence of this use before the Muslim invasion in about AD 1175. Engines for sending missiles from the ramparts, however, were known even to the Ayodhya of the *Ramayana*. Most often mentioned are catapults able to hurl boulders, and crossbows capable of shooting several arrows at once. Reference to *agni curna* (a compound of saltpetre, sulphur and charcoal) in a late treatise has led to extravagant claims for early India as the inventor of gunpowder, but it is probable that this mention was interpolated after the rise of Muslim power in India. Indeed, had guns and gunpowder been known in ancient India, they would have been remarked by all the foreign travellers who left accounts of pre-Muslim times.

By the 4th century BC great metropolitan forts had long been known in India. The most important ones lay between Mathura on the Jumna to Magadha on the lower Ganges, and another series led south from the great Avanti capital of Ujjain across the Narmada at Maheshvar into the Deccan. Amongst the most important remains are the walls and bastions of Rajagriha, and excavations at several other places in the Ganges basin, notably Kaushambhi, have revealed great battered walls of burnt brick, though little of formal planning.

Not unlike that of the gods, the king's walled complex of courts and pavilions (*vimana* or *prasada*) is sometimes referred to as the 'inner town' (*antepura*). Surrounded by administrative offices, the outer palace was dominated by a hall of public audience (*raja bhavana*). Ceremonials took place in one or more outer courts to which the public were admitted through a gatehouse, with a hall for waiting and meeting. Inner courts, often with gardens, served the pavilions of the king's private quarters and the enclosed quarters for the women (*zenana*). In their walled compounds these pavilions were usually multi-storey timber structures of posts and beams (trabeated) on masonry bases. The upper levels contained the living quarters, often arranged in apartments. Perhaps walled only with lattices and lit by windows with grilled shutters (*jalis*), the storeys sometimes stepped

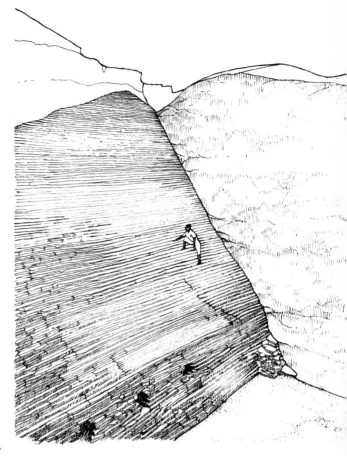

Kushinagara, ancient brick ramparts.

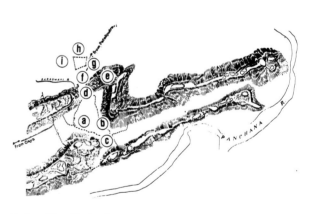

Rajagriha, fort plan:
a. Inner fort
b. East Gate
c. South Gate
d. North Gate
e. Maniyar Math
f. Suraj Kund
g. Bastion
h. Outer fort
i. Burning ghat

13

back with full-length bay-windows opening onto ballustraded terraces often accommodating separate kiosks. The ground floor contained reception and service rooms, sometimes with recessed verandahs or porticos. In the king's palace, private audience was presumably provided for on the ground floor of the principal *prasada*, below his chamber. If there is no complete picture of the 'inner town', the early reliefs show a variety of *prasadas*, regular and irregular, and the frescoes of Ajanta give a timeless image of the *raja bhavana* comparable with the 'Thousand-Pillared Halls' mentioned in the Jatakas, or the great hall of Pataliputra.

Persian craftsmen sought employment at the Mauryan court of Pataliputra following the extinction of Achaemenid patronage and they seem to have provided the setting for the daily round of royal duties, and the ceremonial that went with them, which took place within the king's fort. Mornings were devoted to public audience, with private audience following as occasion required. The provision of distinct multi-columned halls (*apadanas*) for these, in appropriate relationship to the royal apartments, was the continuously evolving concern of Persian royal architects as it was for Indian architects, from the Pataliputra of Chandragupta Maurya and Kautilya to the Shahjahanabad of the Great Moghul and beyond. Megesthenes, the ambassador of Seleucos Nikator to Chandragupta's court, left a celebrated account of Pataliputra: girded by a ditch and a wooden wall with 570 towers and 64 gates, the sumptuous palace was set in gardens and contained a series of *apadanas* with columns decorated in gold and silver. One of these halls is India's earliest large-scale stone structure; excavators have found stone columns polished in the Persian manner and a capital like many in Buddhist reliefs but decorated as at Persepolis.

After the Mauryas, successive invasions of India from west-central Asia were led by the Bactrians, descendants of soldiers left behind by Alexander the Great to found a kingdom on the banks of the Oxus. Their Hellenistic ideals were to have an important impact on India, not least in planning. The Bactrian capital at Taxila (Sirkap), in marked contrast to the Mauryan settlement nearby if not to India's ancient theoretical tradition, was laid out strictly in accordance with the grid principle of Hellenistic town planners elsewhere, its defences embracing an isolated acropolis as in the most typical of both Hellenistic and later Indian situations. There is little trace of the palace of the Bactrian kings, as Sirkap was rebuilt several times by their less cultured Shaka and Parthian successors. The Greek town grid asserted itself throughout India but the Shaka-Parthian palaces, in sharp contrast to the post and beam structures so far encountered, were like those of Assur and Nysa in the Parthian heartland. They had walls and arches and a vaulted space (*liwan*) closed on three sides but open to a court. At Sirkap, walled chambers surround courts and the halls of public and private audience were dominated by raised *liwans*.

Palace building types: prasada, baradari *(Akbar's fort at Allahabad),* liwan *(Sassanian palace at Ctesiphon).*

The indigenous *prasada*, the imported *apadana* (or the *baradari* derived from it) and the *liwan* were thus the basic forms available to the builders of palaces within India's forts for two thousand years. Indian secular building, except for defence, was generally of less durable material than temples, and little that exists today pre-dates the Muslim invasion, even at the seats of the great Gupta, Chalukya,

Pallava or Chola emperors. Yet in a glimpse of what their establishments may have been like, the chronicler of the reign of the emperor Harsha Vardhana in the 7th century describes a camp which conforms in most respects to the ideal town/fort of the *shastras*. Then again, the faithful reproduction of the age-old *prasada* for the Nyakas of latterday Tanjore and Gingee, in coarse but durable materials, and of the equally venerable *apadana* or *baradaris* in forts as diverse as those of Akbar at Allahabad and Tipu Sultan at Seringapatam, speak eloquently of the innate conservatism of India's builders.

Apart from the defenceworks themselves and the palaces, the other essential component of the fort complex in India was the temple – or the mosque. Before the Muslim invasions, except for a small minority of Jains, most Indians were Hindus, devoted to a trinity embracing the cycle of creation, preservation and destruction. The latter two were personified as Vishnu and Shiva and, together with his wife or motivating force (*shakti*), each gained vast followings to the almost total exclusion of the original creator, Brahma. The most important development in Hinduism before AD 500 was the descent of the god from aloofness to care for man through his *shakti*. Vaishnavites, Shaivites and even Jains, who followed the creed of the 7th century BC reformer Mahavira, were largely tolerant of one another, none denying that they worshipped an aspect of a single divinity.

The deity whose grace is invoked for salvation is worshipped through a sanctified image or symbol – the *avatars* (aspects) of Vishnu, the *lingam* (phallus) of Shiva. Worship is not congregational, but primarily the sacrifice of service and sustenance by the individual or by the priest whose caste fits him to represent the community at large. In practice this would require only a chamber to house the image, preceded by a porch to shelter the worshipper and perhaps a pavilion (*mandapa*) for attendants or ritual performers, but the building of the Hindu temple goes far beyond such necessities.

The temple is a place of pilgrimage. Ideally, pilgrimage is to the holy waters, a spiritually purifying fording-place. If water is not naturally present at the site, it is introduced, and represented by a wide range of ancient water-based fertility symbols. The temple is also a place of divine appearance where the god's grace is stimulated in consort with his *shakti*: its centre is called the womb chamber (*garbla griha*), because the gestation of grace takes place there. Thus the site is inseminated and the temple is embellished with statues of the god and goddess complemented by sexually explicit 'loving couples' (*maithunas*).

The place of contact between God and man is identified with the form of the universe: its plan follows sacred mathematical formulae relating to the order of the universe and enshrining the ancient planning rules we have already met. The superstructure (*shikhara*), initially of superimposed slabs, was soon modelled on the multi-storeyed *prasada* as the 'Palace of the Gods'. This was always so in the south, where the storeys of the shrine (*vimana*) have open terraces with kiosks. In the north the superstructure was taken through several abstractions to produce a variety of forms after the image of the cosmic mountain – in general the many-peaked Meru, the abode of the gods, specifically Kailasha of Shiva and Vaikuntha of Vishnu.

After the Muslim invasions, mosques became an integral part of many

Temple at Sunak (Gujarat): left porch, centre mandapa, *right sanctuary with many-peaked* shikhara.

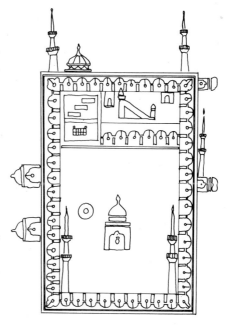

Mosque of the Prophet, Medina (from 16th-century miniature showing court, prayer hall mihrab, *minaret,* mimbar, *tank).*

15

fort complexes. The prime influences of Islam on architecture is prayer, the second Pillar; and the designation of Mecca, the place of Muhammad's birth and Abraham's sacrifice, as the axis of prayer (*qibla*) is the crucial discipline. Fundamental, too, is the Quranic prescription of a precise prayer ritual, including prostration on a mat protecting the worshipper from the impurities of the ground. The mosque (*masjid*) provides for the community's statutory noon prayers on Friday (*Juma*, hence *Juma* or *Jami Masjid*). In an enclosed court, defending worshippers from impurity, the predominant element is the *qibla* wall, marked by a central recession (*mihrab*). Offsetting this is a tower (minaret or *minar*) from which the Muslim is called to prayer. A tank for washing, a lectern for the Quran and a pulpit (*mimbar*) are the essential furniture. Fleeing from the hostile inhabitants of Mecca in AD 622, the Prophet had settled in Medina and founded a mosque there. Simply an adaptation of the courtyard house of which it was an adjunct, a verandah provided shelter to a limited number of worshippers before the *qibla* wall, and another for the Prophet's homeless followers was erected on the opposite side. Virtually all subsequent mosques have retained these elements. Diversity of form has come primarily from the treatment of the prayer hall, sometimes as a series of uninterrupted colonnades or arcades, sometimes with a great central domed space and a façade dominated by a *liwan*.

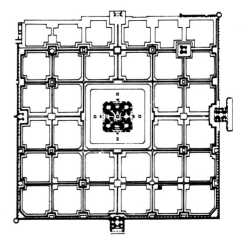

Madrasah *of Mahmud Gawan at Bidar.*

The other Islamic building type which the traveller will encounter at many of the forts described in this book is the tomb and its garden setting. Islam requires burial for the dead. The grave is marked at ground level by a slab reflecting the position of the body below, inscribed with the 99 names of God. After the precedent supposedly set at the grave of the first Caliph, Ali, it was considered meritorious to cover the burial places of holy men (*sufis*) with canopies. Wishing to be buried in the orbit of 'benign influence' (*baraka*), many built tomb chambers for themselves and a *sufi*, while others built free-standing mausoleums, and *baraka* was provided by the setting, the garden (*chahar bagh*). This represented the image of Paradise after the ancient Persian ideal of Order, to which the Quran's Eden is related – an enclosed square divided centrally into four by four rivers flowing in the cardinal directions from the 'Waters of Life'. Though cremated and therefore without graves, Hindus emulated Muslims by erecting memorial canopies (*chattris*) at spots associated with death or cremation and, like Muslim princes, later Hindu rulers brought the *chahar bagh* into their fort-palaces.

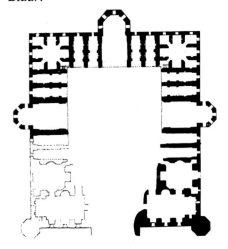

Tomb of Humayun at Dinpanah (Delhi) with chahar bagh.

The use of artillery in Europe from the 14th century fundamentally changed the nature of fortification there. The height and thickness of walls had formerly been crucial, but it was gradually realised that walls must be brought low and sunk into ditches both to present a minimal target and to give cannons command of the approaches. Instead of missiles hurled forward from a great height, saturation coverage by crossfire was essential. With steady improvement in the range and accuracy of firearms, bastions covering one another had to be pushed further out. Their thickness was greatly increased, often by massive battering, but the curved forms effective against sapping were replaced by angular ones to deflect shot.

Apart from the sophistications introduced with artillery, earlier fortifications built in India after the Muslim invasion reflect other developments in the west, notably the *motte* and *bailey* principle developed in the Holy Land by the Crusaders. The great rectangular keep or *donjon*, familiar in France and England, provided a last resort against external assault or internal treachery. It was sometimes isolated within concentric rings of ramparts, but the trend was to transform it into a massive towered structure integrated with the main line of defence. The successive ranges of walls were tiered for maximum coverage in depth. Not to hinder marksmen manning the parapets, the holes (machicolations) through which missiles could be dropped on would-be sappers were grouped behind boxes or hoods, which projected at regular intervals rather than continuously around the curtain.

The isolation of a citadel from a more expansive outwork was highly characteristic of the Muslims in India, as at Bidar or Golconda. It not only reflected the Norman *motte* and *bailey*, but also the venerable practice of establishing a settlement under the protection of a naturally defensible eminence, as familiar to ancient Indian theorists as to the early practitioners from Mohenjo-Daro to Mycenae. It is only the rare exception to this in India, like the wholly man-made stronghold of Gulbarga's *donjon*, which follows from Muslim familiarity with Crusader practice. Apart from their fundamental grasp of all the advantages to be drawn from naturally defensible sites, it is clear from Kautilya that the ancient Indians were familiar with the two basic methods of augmenting them: walls covered by flanking fire from regularly spaced towers; defence in depth provided by concentric rings of walls and moats with advanced outworks controlling the approach. In general the ancient *shastra* tradition has its parallel in Roman theory and practice. In particular the ingenuity shown by Kautilya in devising means to thwart an enemy's advance is certainly equal to the $90°$ turns in the paths through the gates of ancient Greek forts, for example, and in this respect above all Indian castle builders were to prove themselves his worthy heirs.

The passing of the last Hindu emperors of northern India, the Guptas and Harsha Vardhana in the 7th century, left a power vacuum that was not filled until the advent of the Muslims at the end of the 12th century. The Pratiharas came nearest to doing so. They emerged from amongst four clans, generally called Rajputs and tracing their descent from the sun or the moon, which formed the Gujarat tribe that entered India after the Huns; the other three were the Solankis, the Paramaras and the Chauhans. Countering the Arabs in Sind, the Pratiharas captured the former imperial capital, Kanauj, by the end of the 8th century. Exhausted by conflict with other would-be Indian emperors, notably the Palas of Bengal, they were overwhelmed by Mahmud of Ghazni in the 11th century. The Palas were thus able to take Kanauj, but in the mid-12th century they lost their Bengal base to the Senas.

After the fall of the Pratiharas, the Solankis, who had won Gujarat, tried to fill the void, but they were contained in the east by the Paramaras, who had won Malwa, and in the north by the Chauhans, who asserted their dominance over lesser Rajputs in much of modern Rajasthan. Other Rajputs, like the Guhilots of Chitor and Kachhwahas of Amber, sustained a measure of independence, while the Khachhpa-

17

ghatas of Gwalior, the Chandellas of Khajurao and the Kalachuris of Tripur shared former Pratihara or Pala domains in modern Madhya Pradesh. In the Deccan, the Chalukyan empire was divided by the late 12th century between the Yadavas of Devagiri, the Hoysalas of Mysore and the Kakatays of Warangal, and soon afterwards the great Cholas of Tanjore were eclipsed by the Pandyas of Madura.

The beneficiaries of the chaos produced by Indian dynastic rivalry – which was responsible for the astonishing proliferation of forts throughout the sub-continent – were the Muslims. Foremost was Mahmud of Ghazni, but he did not remain. Muhammad Ghuri, another adventurer from Afghanistan, swept in late in the 12th century with different intentions. The following table highlights the major events and characters met with in this book:

1192	Prithviraj Chauhan defeated by Mahmud at the battle of Tarain
1206	Delhi Sultanate founded by Qutb-ud-din Aibak; Iltutmish (1211–27)
1296	Accession to Sultanate of Ala-ud-din Khilji (d. 1316)
1303	Fall of Mewar on Ala-ud-din's capture of Chitor
1320	Accession to Sultanate of Tughluqs; Muhammad bin Tughluq (1325–51)
1326	Sisodias regain Mewar; Rana Kumbha (1433–68); Sanga (1506–28)
1336	Kingdom of Vijayanagar founded; Krishna Deva Raya (1509–30)
1342	Sultanate of Bengal founded
1347	Bahamani kingdom of Gulbarga founded; capital to Bidar 1429
1398	Invasion of Timur (Tamburlaine) and end of Tughluqs
1401	Ghorid Sultunate of Malwa founded; Mahmud Khilji (1436–69)
1410	Sultanate of Gujarat founded
1414–1526	Sayyid and Lodi dynasties of Delhi Sultans
1459	Jodhpur founded as capital of Marwar by Rao Jodha Rathore
1482–1512	Bahmani kingdom disintegrates into independent states of Bidar, Ahmadnagar, Berar, Bijapur, Golconda and Khandesh
1498	Portuguese arrive in India
1501–31	Rudra Pratap Bundela founds Orchha
1526	Babur founds Moghul empire with victory at Panipat
1530–56	Humayun; Afghan Suri Interregnum (1540–55)
1555–1605	Akbar and the conquest of northern India
1565	Vijayanagar destroyed by Muslims after battle of Tarain
1605–27	Jehangir and the beginning of conquest in the Deccan
1612–90	British gain Surat, Madras (1639), Bombay (1661), Calcutta (1690)
1628–58	Shahjahan
1627–80	Shivaji Bhonsale establishes Maratha power
1656–1707	Aurangzeb (Alamgir) and the conquest of southern India

18

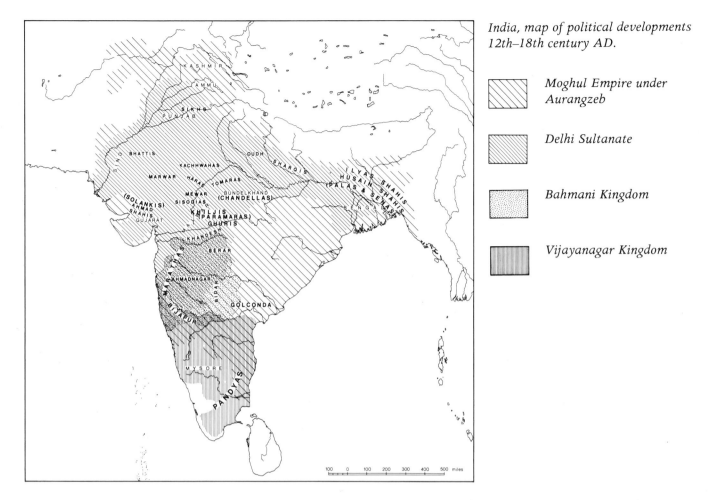

Akbar cemented his empire with tolerance; Aurangzeb undermined it with bigotry. After Bahadur Shah I (1707–12) defeated the Sikhs, decline was rapid till the Marathas and Persians invaded Delhi and humiliated Muhammad Shah in 1738–9. Thereafter the disintegration of the Moghul Empire at the hands of Marathas, Sikhs, former imperial governors and resurgent Rajputs, was rapid. The state of confusion created by these contending forces again left India prey to a superior outside power. With the defeat of the French in the Seven Years' War and of the Nawab of Bengal at Plassey, that power was Britain, and in the struggle that followed many of the forts described in this book played a decisive role for the last time.

The most frequently used architectural names and terms, with which the reader will soon become familiar, are all defined within the index. In the space available to us here, it has not been possible to give a detailed history charting every rise and fall, every striking character, every tale of heroism or treachery associated with the forts, but it is hoped that enough is given to bring to life those buildings which may be seen today. The great set-pieces of Delhi and Agra are of course frequently visited, but many among India's remarkable heritage of fortress-palaces are more remote, in wild and beautiful country. The glories of these bastions and their treasuries will excite the mind and stir the emotions of any traveller.

Purana Qila west gate.

'If there is a Paradise on Earth, it is this, it is this, it is this.' So proclaimed Shahjahan, fifth Moghul Emperor of India, in letters of gold upon the ceiling of his throne room in the Red Fort.

Shahjahan's great 17th-century creation was the last of Delhi's famed 'seven cities', not including those earlier swept away by the holy river Jumna, nor Lutyens' much later new capital of British India. After consultations with astrologers, the foundations were laid in 1638, and ten years later nine extravagant days of celebration marked the Emperor's entry into Shahjahanabad, the 'City of the Ruler of the World'. The magnificent fortress-palace of finely dressed red sandstone measures 3200 by 1600 feet. Rising to 100 feet in places, the thick, battlemented walls, relieved by string courses and cusped parapets, are reinforced at regular intervals with massive round bastions, and surrounded by a deep moat.

The splendid Delhi and Lahore Gates were ultimately given barbicans to deflect an enemy's line of approach through a right-angled turn, but though the decline and fall of the Moghul Empire began and ended in the Red Fort, it was far less a scene of siege and sack, far more a treasure house of spendour and beauty for the victors.

Shahjahan himself formed the Red Fort's general design, but its construction was overseen by two Persian brothers, Ahmad and Hamid ul-Asar. The Lahore Gate, with its octagonal guard chamber, opens the main road from the west; the Delhi Gate, west of centre in the south, opens another road through a bazaar. These two axes cross in a great square court before the Naubat Khana gatehouse leading to the Diwan-i-Am, the Hall of Public Audience.

Fifty feet long and 24 wide, with a 10-foot open verandah all around, the hall was a place of overwhelming majesty, its 32 sandstone columns plastered with powdered marble, its roof encased in silver foliage with gold inlay. On the raised platform on the eastern side, beneath a *bangaldar baldachino* of white marble and Italian *pietra dura*, was the durbar seat, the 'Seat of the shadow of God', Shahjahan's Peacock Throne. Made of gem-encrusted gold on six massive solid gold feet, the throne took its name from two peacock figures standing behind it, their tails expanded and inlaid with sapphires, rubies, emeralds and other precious stones. It was surmounted by a canopy of gold and rubies, supported by twelve colonnettes richly emblazed with costly gems, and bearing a fringe made of pearls. The throne was the work of the French jeweller, Austin Bordeaux, and was rumoured to have cost 150 million francs.

Before the throne was a dais from which the Grand Wazir handed petitions up to the Emperor. In attendance, strictly ranked, were all the officers of State – the greatest nobles in the hall itself, the rest in descending order ranged in enclosures in the court defined by ropes of gold, silver and red silk. The daily scene in the Red Fort was gorgeous enough; on special occasions, such as the Emperor's birthday, there were displayed unparalleled opulence of costly dress, gold, silver and ivory, plumes, parasols and palanquins, richly caparisoned elephants and horses.

The garden court to the east of the throne platform leads to a series of exquisitely chased and inlaid marble pavilions for the court on the riverside terrace, the first of which is the Rang Mahal, its crenellated

The Red Fort, early 19th-century ink and watercolour panorama from the Jumna river.

The Red Fort Lahore Gate.

baluster-like columns recalling the reed-bundle piers of Bengal.
Running through them all is the Nahar-i-Behist, the Canal of Paradise,
using water raised from the river in the north-east bastion. The canal
supplied the baths, and flowed on through delicate pools and fountains
culminating in the sumptuous *padma* (lotus) fountain of the Rang
Mahal. The gardens of the Red Fort, always an important part of
Moghul life, were made possible by the presence of water. Its cooling
effect, its sensuous rippling over white marble, would have subtly
stressed the carved perfection – roses, jasmine and lilies – of the
women's quarters. The Hayat Baksha garden pavilions had niches for
candles, over which the water would cascade.

Shahjahan owed these waterworks to Ali Mardan Khan, once
Governor of Kandahar for the Shah of Persia. Suspected of embezzle-
ment of State revenues and no doubt fearing for his safety, Ali Mardan
quietly delivered his province to the Moghuls and began a new career
for them as a talented engineer. Shahjahan later lost Kandahar back to
the Persians, a loss he faced with equanimity in the tranquil, poised
beauty of his water pavilions.

Shahjahan is known to have reviewed the plans for Baghdad when
designing his Red Fort, and like the palaces of the great Caliphs, his
buildings are aligned north–south to avoid any discordance with the
qibla wall, facing Mecca, of his mosques. He used marble – the finest

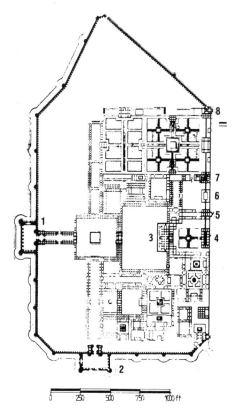

22

OPPOSITE *The Red Fort Delhi Gate.*

Plan of the Red Fort:
1. Lahore Gate
2. Delhi Gate
3. Diwan-i-Am
4. Rang Mahal
5. Khas Mahal
6. Diwan-i-Khas
7. Baths
8. Hayat Baksha

ABOVE *Diwan-i-Am, the Hall of Public Audience, showing the raised platform and canopy which once housed the Peacock Throne.*

ABOVE RIGHT *Rang Mahal, the lotus fountain and the 'Canal of Paradise'.*

Diwan-i-Khas, the Hall of Private Audience.

Moti Masjid, the Pearl Mosque.

A marble screen in the Khas Mahal.

25

Makrana marble from Jodhpur, with its delicate graining and artfully inlaid with semi-precious stones, for his Diwan-i-Khas, the Private Audience Chamber, for the Khas Mahal and the Musamman Burj, an octagonal tower with its projecting *jharokha*, place of appearance, which was used once more for its original purpose by the King-Emperor George V during the Delhi Durbar of 1912, to review the vast pageantry passing below. The white marble Moti Masjid, the Pearl Mosque, was begun late in Shahjahan's reign and completed by his successor, Aurangzeb.

In 1657 Shahjahan, increasingly remote from the affairs of State, fell ill. His four sons, already experienced as semi-independent governors of powerful regions and armies, commenced a bloody war of succession. Shahjahan supported his eldest son, Dara Shikoh, but in a great battle at Agra in 1659, Aurangzeb proved victor. Cool and ruthless, Aurangzeb lost no time in despatching brothers and nephews to perdition, but not his father: Shahjahan ended his days a prisoner in Agra Fort.

The 50 years after Aurangzeb's death in 1707 saw nine crowned heads fall: by then the blinding and murder of emperors had become almost commonplace against a background of chaotic jostling for power by Persian, Afghan and Maratha armies. In 1739 Nadir Shah of Persia defeated Muhammad Shah. Though he left Muhammad Shah as Moghul, Nadir Shah ordered a general massacre of Delhi's population in reprisal for the murder of some of his Persians. He left Delhi with the imperial treasury – jewels, pearls, diamonds, including the Koh-i-nur, gold, silver, camels, horses, elephants – and the Peacock Throne; and he left behind a regime fatally weakened by carnage and continuing dissension.

The hundred years between the Battle of Plassey and the Great Indian Mutiny knew three Moghul emperors, though by 1857 there was no empire left. In the British relief – and reduction – of Delhi, it seemed for a time as if the Red Fort might sink into disuse and obscurity

Qutb Minar, Victory Tower.

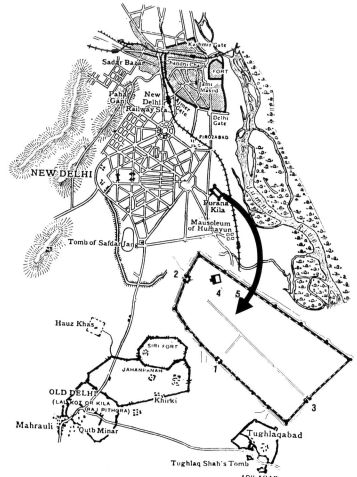

Plan of Delhi and the Purana Qila
(inset)
1. West Gate
2. North Gate
3. South Gate
4. Qila-i-Khuna
5. Sher Mandal

28

as had so many of its predecessors: the great, battered, triple-tiered walls of 14th-century Tughlaqabad, keeping empty watch over the tiny island citadel of its ruler's tomb; the astonishing red sandstone Qutb Minar, Tower of Victory, built by Ala-ud-din Khilji in the 13th century; Firozabad, its 14th-century pavilions recalling the tent-palaces of central Asia; and the citadel of the second great Moghul, Humayun, dominated by the Purana Qila – great portals set into powerful bastions of contrasting tilework, marble mosaic and sandstone. Within it stands the octagonal Sher Mandal, used by Humayun as a library, where he fell accidentally to his death; and the fine Qila-i-Khuna mosque of richly coloured stone and inlaid marble.

But builders may cross the bridges of time where empires cannot. Lutyens used the 16th-century Purana Qila as an inspiration for his New Delhi, echoing the great days of the Red Fort and the intentions of its creator: 'Shahjahan evinced, in the construction of these gardens, the same taste for picturesque beauty and sublimity as he did in building and other works of art. Here every provision was made to render seclusion pleasant, to gratify the senses, to soften the cares of royalty, and to beguile the tedium of life.'

ABOVE *Sher Mandal, where Humayun fell to his death.*

Qila-i-Khuna Mosque.

AGRA

Like Caesar who found Rome built of bricks, Shahjahan replaced much of Agra's red sandstone with sumptuous white marble. For the first half of his reign he governed mostly from Agra. For twenty years he stayed here, overseeing the construction of the supreme masterpiece of the epoch, the tomb of his adored queen Mumtaz Mahal, the legendary Taj Mahal. Deposed by his son Aurangzeb, Shahjahan returned to spend his last seven years, helpless and in poor health, in the fort of Agra. Imprisoned in the Musamman Burj, he could command a view of the incomparable Taj, and gazed towards it on his deathbed. He is buried alongside his queen.

Agra was the capital of Shahjahan's grandfather, Akbar. He had succeeded his father, Humayun, as an ambitious thirteen-year-old and in twenty years his empire stretched from Kabul to the Deccan, from Bengal to Gujarat with its control over trade with western Asia, Africa and the Portuguese. Founded on a sophisticated administrative system, on religious toleration and on flourishing trade, the empire was embellished by one of the world's great schools of art, centred on Akbar's Red Fort at Agra on the Jumna.

Work on this began in 1564 on a scale never before attempted, a mile and a half in circuit. On the river side, a broad terrace lies between the two-tiered walls with irregularly spaced bastions, one of which, the most prominent, commands a water gate leading to a network of underground passages. On the town side, the moated doubled and bastioned walls are more massive and rise to over 100 feet, with at least two rows of slits for marksmen.

The site had long been a stronghold. Mahmud of Ghazni, the early 11th-century scourge of the Hindus in north-west India, stormed a strong fort here, but the Rajputs won it back again. The last of the Delhi Sultans had their capital here at the end of the 15th century, and the first of the Moghuls, Babur, sent his son Humayun to occupy Agra. This he did, capturing the Rajah of Gwalior and his family. They were spared; their gratitude took the form of jewels and precious stones, among them the diamond that came to be known as the Koh-i-nur, the mountain of light. Humayun lost his empire for twenty years to the Afghan, Sher Shah, and Akbar was born on the road to exile.

Sher Shah spent a year in Agra and carried out repairs to the old fort and the city. Akbar's building schemes took eight years and according to the official record of the construction, he added 'upwards of 500 edifices of red stone in the fine styles of Bengal and Gujarat'.

The main entrance to Akbar's fort is the Delhi Gate to the west, the first monumental gate of the Moghuls. The twin-towered Hathi Pol, the Elephant Gate, took its name from two elephants of stone on pedestals to either side of the portal, destroyed later by Aurangzeb to eradicate any Hindu appearance. Akbar's liberal tolerance was every-

Taj Mahal from Musamman Burj in the Red Fort, where Shahjahan was imprisoned.

30

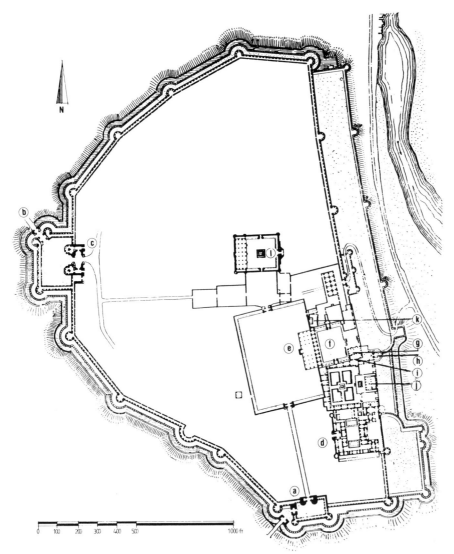

Plan of Agra fort:
a. Amar Singh Gate
b. Delhi Gate
c. Hathi Pol
d. Jehangiri Mahal
e. Diwan-i-Am
f. Machli Bhawan
g. Diwan-i-Khas
h. Musamman Burj
i. Khas Mahal and Anguri Bagh
j. Shish Mahal

The Red Fort from the river front.

where displayed in a synthesis of building styles: Islamic calligraphic and geometric decorations, Hindu motifs of flora and fauna. The Delhi Gate contains the *gajvyala*, the elephant panel, displaying the surrender of seven elephants to symbolise the indestructible power of the empire. The elephants were overcome by a hybrid winged beast, reminiscent of the Assyrian griffin but comparable to the monsters of Hindu temple architecture, with the neck and ears of a horse, the legs and tail of a lion, the tusks and trunk of an elephant. It is fighting with all seven elephants at once: four under the claws, one thrown in the air, one held wrapped in the tail and another in the trunk.

The Amar Singh Gate to the south is defended by two barbicans. The main portal has an elegant gallery and blind arcading in superimposed tiers, enhancing the sense of height, though the turrets are no taller than the battlements. The gate was named during Shahjahan's reign after one of the sons of the Maharaja of Jaipur. Reprimanded by the Emperor in the Diwan-i-Am, reached through the gate, for being absent from court without permission on a hunting expedition, he went berserk and cut down several nobles standing near the throne, and lunged at the Emperor himself before being felled by his own brother-in-law. Amar Singh's retainers, dressed in saffron robes, went on a rampage, killing many before they themselves were killed. His widow, a princess from Bundi, committed *suttee*, burning on her husband's pyre.

Not many of Akbar's '500 edifices' remain. One which does is the Jehangiri Mahal in the *zenana* compound. This is completely Hindu in character, and was clearly influenced by the Gwalior Man Mandir: halls, arched recesses, pillars, on two levels, pavilions above ground and *serdabs* below, all linked by well-guarded underground passages. The decoration is marvellous: capitals of wheels and flowers, others of a ribbed leaf design like an acanthus, ornamental carvings of birds and fruit, elaborately adorned doors and windows, brilliant stucco and fresco work, sculptures of elephants wearing bells. There had been many Hindu dancing girls and concubines but Akbar married a Rajput princess from Amber and made her his queen, allowing her to practise her religion in the *zenana* and have a temple in the palace. The orthodox Muslims among Akbar's 300 wives and 5000 concubines found it hard to reconcile themselves to the fact that their future emperor, her son, would be part infidel. Tolerance came in some measure in time but there was much opposition when Akbar decided to end the *jizya* tax on Hindus, and even joined in Hindu festivals in his *zenana*.

Imperial proceedings in the Diwan-i-Am, the Hall of Public Audience, could be watched by the women of the *zenana*. Affairs of State were dealt with in the Diwan-i-Khas, the Hall of Private Audience. Between the two was a magnificent garden, the Machli Bhawan or Fish Square,

Amar Singh Gate and battlements.

with marble fountains and tanks full of fish; now only the cloistered court remains.

Close to the Jehangiri Mahal is the court of the sumptuous Khas Mahal, with its twin Bengali-style gilded Naulakhi kiosks. In these were retiring rooms for the ladies of the court, with deep holes in the walls into which they used to slip their jewels, so narrow that only a woman's hand could withdraw the contents. Nearby, too, is the Anguri

Bagh, the Garden of Grapes, named for the carving on its cloisters. For this exquisite *chahar bagh*, soil was brought from Kashmir, and water coursed through marble into jasper. Between the courts of the Khas Mahal and the Diwan-i-Khas was the Shish Mahal, the Palace of Mirrors, communicating with the baths and the elegant Musamman Burj decorated with fresco and inlay work in marble, with a splendid *chattri* and fountain. The Burj also had a courtyard with squares of black and white marble, used by the Rajputs for playing *pachisi*, a form of back-gammon.

The Moti Masjid, the Pearl Mosque, lies beyond the Diwan-i-Am, an open-sided prayer hall and court on a raised terrace at the highest point of the fort. Fulfilling the role of chapel to the court was the exquisite Nagina Masjid, the Gem Mosque. All these buildings bear the spectacularly lavish hallmark of Shahjahan, cusped arcading in white marble inlaid with semi-precious stones.

In his younger days Akbar had revelled in the Mongol sport where soldiers fanned out in thick forests beating drums to drive hundreds of animals into a concentration for the slaughter. In one such gathering, which lasted weeks, 15,000 animals were killed. The butchery was not entirely without purpose: it was believed that the skills required for hunting improved horsemanship and quick decision-making, and above all tested men's nerve when faced with danger and bloodshed.

Elephant fighting was a favourite court entertainment, usually taking place below the fort walls on the banks of the Jumna, with the Emperor and his ladies watching from the terrace of the Jehangiri Mahal. Abu-l Fazl, Akbar's friend and confidant, describes a bout between Girandar, belonging to Akbar's eldest son Prince Salim, and

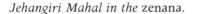
Jehangiri Mahal in the zenana.

Peacock arches in the Diwan-i-Am,
the Hall of Public Audience.

36

Khas Mahal with Bengali golden-roofed pavilions overlooking the Jumna.

A marble fountain in Shish Mahal.

*Khas Mahal and court of the Anguri
Bagh – the Garden of Grapes – in the*
zenana.

Arup, the elephant of Prince Khusru. The whole court watched the
mighty tuskers go at each other, their ivory double-strapped with gold.
Arup was badly mauled and Salim's supporters stoned a third elephant
always kept in reserve to help an injured beast; a general brawl
developed between the rival princes and their men. The maddened
elephants were somehow separated by fireworks but, quite out of
control, they leapt into the Jumna.

Shocked and furious, the ageing Akbar fell ill soon after this and his
health declined still further when he heard that Salim was implicated
in the murder of Abu-l Fazl. In 1605 Akbar died. Prince Salim succeeded
him as the Emperor Jehangir and built his father's tomb at Sikandra, a
few miles from the Agra Fort. Terraces, fountains, flowerbeds, aque-
ducts – all are beautifully proportioned. Jehangir built here in his
father's memory the first minarets in India since the Qutb Minar at
Delhi, four centuries earlier.

FATEHPUR SIKRI

'Tis all a Chequer-board of
   Nights and days
Where Destiny with Men
   for pieces plays:
Hither and Thither moves,
   and mates and slays,
And one by one back in the
   Closet lays.

OMAR KHAYYAM

Like the cactus flower that for a moment adorns the desert, so was Fatehpur Sikri's brief span of glory. Abandoned after only fifteen years through lack of water, today its great buildings stand before the traveller almost untouched by the passage of time.

Akbar had come to regard Agra as unlucky for him in one respect: no heir had been born to him there. A *sufi* saint, Sheikh Salim Chishti, who had chosen Sikri, high on a ridge more than twenty miles west of Agra, as his *khangah* or retreat, prophesied that Akbar would have three sons. The prophecy was fulfilled: a first son was named Salim in honour of the saint. Akbar began to build a palace at Sikri for his Rajput queen, and on his return from a thanksgiving pilgrimage to the shrine of the *sufi* order's founder at Ajmer, he announced that the new city, nearly seven miles in circumference, would be his capital. After the conquest of Gujarat in 1573, it was named Fatehpur, Victory Town. Little remains of the town today except the bazaar.

The fortified palace was built on the ridge, its sumptuous pavilions dispersed, in accordance with the traditions of Akbar's Timurid ancestors, around a central walled garden and broad terrace. Later, *pachisi* and chess-related games were played here, reputedly with naked slave girls as pawns.

The Diwan-i-Am was reached by the people through a triple gate from the market place between the Agra Gate in the north-east and the Naubat Khana, where the imperial band would announce the Emperor's daily audience. To its north is the celebrated free-standing pavilion with deep *chadyas* or eaves, and elegant *chattris* or canopies, thought to have been the Diwan-i-Khas. Its outstanding feature is the central pillar, with a fantastic capital of radiating serpentine brackets, that bears a circular platform with bridges to the surrounding gallery.

The Emperor would enter his red sandstone palace through the Hathi Pol at the north of the city, once framed by life-size stone elephants with intertwined trunks. Nearby were the imperial cara-

A general view showing Panch Mahal, Haram Sara and the Imperial Mosque.

41

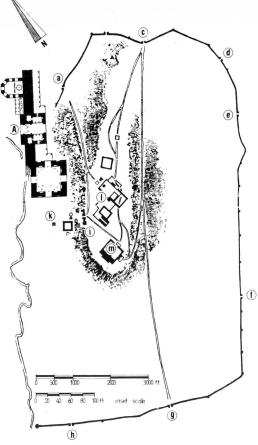

Plan of Fatepur Sikri:

a. Delhi Gate
b. Lal Gate
c. Agra Gate
d. Birbal Gate
e. Chandanpal Gate
f. Gwalior Gate
g. Tenra Gate
h. Ajmer Gate
i. Hathi Pol (and inset A)
j. Caravanserai
k. Hiran Minar
l. Palace
m. Jami Masjid

vanserai and polo ground, and an artificial lake that may have been planned by Akbar's grandfather, Babur, after he subdued the Rajputs of Sikri in the 12th century. The lake and over a mile of walls with eight twin-towered gates protected the town of Fatehpur Sikri – or would have, had the wall been completed. Also near at hand is the Hiran Minar or Deer Minaret, said to have been erected over the grave of Akbar's favourite elephant, and from which he would shoot at driven antelope and other game. The five-tiered Panch Mahal, once gloriously screened to ensure a secluded link between the Emperor's court and his *zenana*, dominates the entire Haram Sara compound. The first floor is remarkable for its 56 columns which support the storey above: no two are alike in design. Close at hand is the ladies' Nagina Masjid and their gardens; to the north are an elegant Hawa Mahal, a breeze chamber, and a screened viaduct giving them access to pleasure pavilions by the water.

Akbar's private, water-cooled apartments were to the south of the compound. He would have rested on the top floor of the principal *baradari* or pillared pavilion, worked in the richly painted cabinet below, and probably held private audience in the adjoining dais-chamber. A single gate leads to the large quadrangle of the Haram Sara, and apartments were provided in wings separated by pavilions of grand reception rooms, all enriched with Gujarati carving of mainly Hindu motifs, and Multani azure blue tiles.

In gratitude to Sheikh Salim, Akbar built for him the great imperial mosque, truly a Moghul masterpiece. It is dominated by the multi-coloured stone Buland Darwaza or Lofty Portal, which probably commemorates Akbar's conquest of Gujarat. Within the mosque's courtyard is Sheikh Salim's white marble tomb: fine screens and extravagant

serpentine brackets springing from chevron-patterned columns below pronounced *chadyas*. With the origins of Fatehpur Sikri so auspicious for childbirth, the Emperor's ladies would tie prayer threads to the ornate screens.

Akbar explored various theologies during his lifetime, and in 1580 he brought to Fatehpur Sikri two Jesuit priests. His obvious lack of adherence to Islam helped bring about a rebellion, and when Akbar marched in 1581 nearly all the influential Muslims in his empire confronted him – defeat would have meant the loss of everything. He returned to auspicious Fatehpur Sikri triumphant, none daring to oppose him again from then until the end of his life.

FAR LEFT *The central carved red sandstone pillar of the throne room, with a fantastic capital of radiating serpentine brackets, supports the throne platform in the Diwan-i-Khas, the Emperor's quarters.*

LEFT *The Imperial Mosque prayer court.*

BELOW *The marble tomb of Sheikh Salim Chisti.*

A screen on which prayer threads are tied by women hoping for fertility.

CHITORGARH

From times when forth from the sunlight
The first of our Kings came down,
And had the earth for his footstool
And wore the stars for his crown.

A still silence hangs over the deserted pavilions and ruined temples of Chitorgarh. Three times in its history, the Sisodia princes of Mewar led their warriors from its walls to carry death to the besiegers or meet it in the field. Three times they left behind them the terrible *johar*, the voluntary immolation of their women and children. Death for all before dishonour.

The fort was never easy to take. Five hundred feet above the plain, the walls of Chitor are the finest mediaeval Hindu defencework to survive in any degree of completeness. Though the merlons in the crenellation have a typically Muslim 'pointed arch' profile, the embrasures splay out from narrow slits below a string course to produce rare wedge-shaped forms. There is one northern gate and four on the

Extensive ruins of Chitorgarh viewed from the south over Gaumukha Tank, and the 'Mahasati' where the two 16th-century johars took place.

LEFT *Rani Padmini's Palace.*

*Ramparts and Rana Kumbha's
Palace viewed from the north.*

Suttee *stones.*

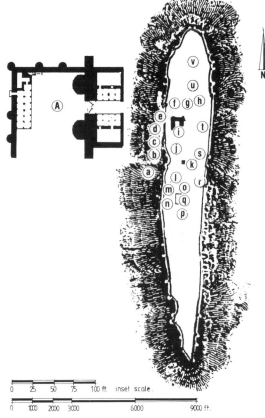

46

eastern wall. But the main approach is from the west and here, across the sinuous route, are seven massive gates: Badal, Bhairon, Hanuman, Ganesha, Jarlan, Lakhama and, finally, the vast Ram Pol, built in 1459 on a richly moulded base of three friezes like those of the Hindu temples. There are no barbicans, but a *mandapa*, a temple hall provided shelter for the guard. Crosswalls link the second, fourth, fifth and sixth gates to the main ramparts.

The heights of Chitor were the key to Rajasthan and its occupation was the first objective of any would-be potentate. Early in the 8th century the Guhilot Bappa Rawal overthrew the Mori ruler there. The Guhilots were dislodged in the 9th century by the Pratiharas; they in turn gave way to the Rashtrakutas and the Paramaras. The Guhilots late in the 11th century wrested Chitor back again, only to become subject to the Solankis of Gujarat and the Tughluqs. Then the Sisodia Guhilots – Suryavanshis, descendants of the sun – expelled the Muslims and Chitor remained theirs until its final sack in 1568 by Akbar.

In 1303, when young Rana Lakhuar Singh was the reigning chief of Mewar, the Sultan of Delhi, the Tartar Ala-ud-din Khilji, laid siege to Chitorgarh. After months of deadlock the Sultan offered to lift the siege on one condition: that he be allowed a glimpse of the fabled beauty of Padmini, wife of the Rana's regent and uncle. The Rajputs finally agreed, but the Sultan was not to be permitted to gaze directly on Padmini – he might see her reflection only.

The palace of Padmini stands in a pool of water. Softly she trod the steps down to the water's edge; rippling in a gentle breeze, slowly it stilled to reveal her lovely face to the Sultan, waiting above. Her husband then escorted his noble guest to Chitor's outer gate; but Ala-ud-din had hidden men among the bushes and Rana Bhim Singh was ambushed and carried away to the enemy lines. The price for his

ABOVE *The Hall of the Guards viewed through Ram Pol.*

RIGHT *Ganesha Pol, the fourth gate.*

Plan of Chitargarh:
 a. Badal Gate (and inset A)
 b. Bhairon Gate
 c. Hanuman Gate
 d. Ganesha Gate
 e. Jarlan and Lakhama Gates
 f. Ram Pol
 g. Srinagar Chauri
 h. Sat Bis Devra Temple
 i. Rana Kumbha's Palace
 j. Maha Sati
 h. Tower of Victory
 l. Samidhishwar Temple
m. Gaumukha Tank
 n. Karika Matha Temple
 o. Surya Temple
 p. Padmini's Palace
 q. Ratan Jenana
 r. Bhimlat
 s. Suraj Gate
 t. Tower of Fame

47

freedom was the hand of the fair Padmini.

Ram Pol, the seventh gate.

Exultant, Ala-ud-din learned that she would come to him, provided she might bring her court of ladies. Under cover of their palanquins, a body of Rajput warriors entered the Sultan's camp. In the battle the Rana and Padmini escaped but his followers died almost to a man.

Ala-ud-din savagely renewed his attack on Chitor. Before the final charge, 'the funeral pyre was lighted within the great subterranean retreat in chambers impervious to the light of day, and the defenders of Chitor beheld in procession the queens, their own wives and daughters, to the number of several thousands. The fair Padmini closed the throng . . . They were conveyed to the cavern and the opening closed upon them.'

Each time Chitor fell, the Sisodia heir was smuggled out in the hope that one day the prince would return to redeem his house. Legend said that Chitorgarh could only be defended by royalty. Hamira, grandson of the Rana, brought off an extraordinary coup to regain possession of the fort. Once more the great *nakkaras*, the huge kettledrums that proclaimed for miles around the exit and entrances of the Ranas, heralded a Sisodia prince. Once more the standard of Mewar, a brilliant solar disk, flew from the ramparts.

Timur destroyed the last of the imperial Tughluq dynasty. Among

*The Jain temple of Shantinath,
Srinagara-Khauri.*

BELOW *Detail of the sumptuous
sculpture of the Samadhishwara
Temple.*

others, Sultan Mahmud of Malwa then withdrew his allegiance to Delhi and cast covetous eyes on Chitor, a prize indeed now, for tin and silver had been discovered there, and the wealth of the Ranas beckoned.

Rana Kumbha forged the warring Rajput clans into a powerful confederacy; he took the field with 100,000 archers and horsemen and 1400 elephants. To commemorate his victory over Mahmud in 1458 he built the famous Jayastambha, the Tower of Victory. Nine storeys and 120 feet high, each tier, a *mandapa* for its associated temple and enriched with balconied windows, is carved profusely with the gods of the Hindu pantheon, yet never at any point does the decoration inter-

Saffron-clad devotees at the portal of the Kumbhashyama Temple.

fere with the outline or design of the building. Many priceless inscriptions inside were later destroyed but one remains: 'Sparkling like the first rays of the sun, the tower rose like the bride of the earth.'

Rana Kumbha's palace is typically Hindu. The principal entrance is to the east into a stable court past a guard house. Beyond is the *durbar* court, beyond that the private apartments and, secure at its heart, the *zenana*. Age-old tradition of the *prasada* is revived in the multi-storeyed wings with their balconies and terraces, and many earlier remains were incorporated into the 15th-century rebuilding, like the Kumbhashyama Temple and, standing by the tank or Gaumukha Kund, the Samidhishwar Temple. There are several Jain shrines from between the 11th and 14th centuries, including the Mahadeva and Shantinath Temples, intricately carved with gods and goddesses, celestial dancers and musicians caught in attitudes of bliss from joy at their music-making.

Rana Kumbha was murdered by his son Udai but he, as if by divine providence, was struck down by lightning. In 1509 Kumbha's grandson, Rana Sangram Singh, 'War Lion', took control in Mewar. Rana Sanga, as he was known, was adored by his people, admired by his nobles and, like his grandfather, united the Rajputs against their many enemies. He hoped even to restore Hindu rule in India, lost in the 12th century with the defeat of Prithviraj Chauhan at Tarain. But he did not know then that Babur, descendant of Timur and of Ghenghis Khan, was trekking across the Hindu Kush in search of an empire. Babur defeated the Delhi Sultan and the Afghans, then turned to contend with the desert Rajputs. At Khanua in 1527 Babur conquered, rallying his men with a call for *jehad*, holy war, to the death. Wounded, Sanga retired to the hills but died the following year, defeat unavenged.

In 1535 Bahadur Shah, Sultan of Gujarat, assaulted Chitorgarh. The Rajmata, the queen mother, attired in martial robes, led a cavalry attack and died fighting with the flower of Rajput nobility. Thirteen thousand women and children made Chitor's second *johar*. Queen Kalaviti, before she died, had sent to Humayun, now Emperor, for help. He arrived too late but drove out Bahadur Shah and gallantly restored Chitor to the Sisodias. By a strange twist of irony, it was Humayun's son, Akbar, who finally destroyed them.

Two young knights, the Rathore Jaimal of Bednore and Patta of Kelwa, 15 and 16 years old, commanded Chitor's defence against Akbar, in the absence of Udai Singh, who had fled. Immortalised in songs and poems, Jaimal was killed by Akbar himself while Patta, dressed in saffron, with his mother and young wife died fighting in the final charge. For Chitor's third *johar* the women dressed in their bridal finery: a swirl of silken skirts, a toss of perfumed plait, the soft sound of ankle bells. Having sent their children before them to die, willing or not, princesses and queens entered the flames. All that was beautiful and vibrant died with them.

Akbar in his rage was bent on an exemplary sack to break the independence of the Rajputs: every building was defaced, every vestige of grandeur destroyed or carried back to Agra, and 30,000 of the country people who had taken part in the defence were put to the sword. The Sisodias never came back. Chitorgarh, scene for a thousand years of heroic valour, romance and adventure, was left desolate, to become the haunt of tigers.

The Tower of Victory rises unblemished into the sky, an ironic comment on the surrounding ruins.

KUMBHALGARH

Mewari gypsies at the foot of the massive fort walls housing Rana Kumbha's Palace.

The walls of Kumbhalgarh are 'more the work of giants than of men', comparable in their grandeur to the Great Wall of China. Deep within the ranges of the Aravallis, the fort commands the pass between the kingdoms of Mewar to the east and Marwar to the west. For 1400 years the Mewars ruled here, fiercest and proudest of the fighting Rajput clans, the longest uninterrupted dynasty in the world, claiming their descent from the sun and Lord Rama.

Tradition ascribes a 2nd-century Jain origin to Kumbhalgarh but its history begins in the mid-16th century with Rana Kumbha, winning the fort from its Mer ruler who offered himself as a sacrifice to strengthen the foundations. Kumbha was a great builder – he built 32 of the 84 forts that girdle Sisodia Mewar – and here he made many additions, including, on the highest point, the Badal Mahal, the Palace of Clouds. To this palace Kumbha brought the lovely princess of Jhalawar, abducted from the castle at Mundore of her betrothed, a Rathore prince of Marwar. He tried to rescue her, undeterred by the thick brush surrounding Kumbhalgarh, but returned in failure: 'Often, when the dust had settled after a monsoon shower, the towers of Kumbhalgarh could be seen from the castle of Mundore, and the light radiated from the chamber of the fair through the gloom of a night in Bhadon to the hall where he brooded o'er his sorrows.'

Rana Kumbha's palace commands the citadel but nearby, rising even higher and perfectly preserved, with friezes of painted elephants, the courts and pavilions of a much later yellow ochre palace draw the gaze. Kumbha encouraged all the fine arts and was himself a poet. Sitting on

the balcony of his Badal Mahal, monsoon clouds swirling through the open pavilions, he wrote verses of love and praise to the Lord Krishna, and composed the music for them. It was here that he was murdered, by his own son.

Inextricably linked with Kumbhalgarh is the story of Panna Dai, nurse to Udai Singh, infant son of Rana Sanga of Chitor. Panna learned of a plot to kill the child, and to save her royal charge substituted her own son in place of the sleeping Udai Singh. The intruders demanded of her the whereabouts of the prince. Unflinchingly she pointed to her sleeping boy, and saw him done to death. Panna smuggled Udai Singh to Kumbhalgarh, where he was brought up as a nephew of the governor. Thirteen years later in the Badal Mahal, amid joyous celebration, took place the *tika* ceremony, the anointing of Prince Udai Singh as the ruler of Mewar. That same year, at the oasis fort of Umarkot in the Great Thar, a child was born who would one day bring down Udai Singh from his glory and destroy Chitor: Akbar, whose birth in exile was celebrated only by the spreading of musk upon the desert air.

After the sacking of Chitor, Akbar also made an attempt on Kumbhalgarh, in 1568. From the Tara Burj sentinels kept watch for his army, for camouflage was easy in the dense undergrowth surrounding the fort. Seven gates barred the way. The first, Arait Pol, is so situated that mirror signals could be flashed to strategic points in the fort. Akbar's forces reached only as far as the second gate, Hulla Pol, pockmarked by his artillery. The third gate is Hanuman Pol, brought to Kumbhalgarh by Rana Kumbha after his own successful siege of Nagaur. From the fourth gate, Bhaivana Pol, a winding path paved with uneven stones leads to the Paghra Pol, its name conjuring up the prancing steeds of the Rajput warriors as they gathered before a charge. Tope Khana Pol housed the cannon and beyond that lies the last gate, the Nimboo Pol, Gate of the Lemon Trees.

The fields within the vast acreage of Kumbhalgarh are irrigated and cultivated today by villagers who have made their home among the old houses; in fact, a busy rural life continues here. *Suttee* stones are frequently found in the fields, evidence that Kumbhalgarh eventually fell to besieging Muslims and not to any rival Rajput clan.

In every fort there is always one temple that is kept alive, attended by an old *pujari*, or priest. Among Kumbhalgarh's 365 temples the most important stands at the entrance, a temple to the goddess Chammunda; behind it is the shrine to the Mer ruler whom Kumbha conquered and, nearby, a beautiful *chattri* of the ruling family, with pillars and domes intact. At the first gate stands the Kila Dttari, the Keeper of the Fort, still revered and lovingly acknowledged by the colourful Mewari gypsies and Kumbhalgarh's villagers.

In time Akbar's son, Prince Salim, captured Kumbhalgarh. The fort

OPPOSITE *Broad ramparts and one of the 365 temples within the fort.*

Bastions on splayed bases seen from below.

55

was not won but lost – Rana Pratep, son of Udai Singh, had to abandon it when the water supply became infested with insects in the rainy season. In the final skirmish for Kumbhalgarh the chief bard of Mewar was killed, but his ballads of romance and heroism echo even now in Rajasthan.

The main gate with doors spiked against elephants.

The crenellated battlements.

JODHPUR

Marusthali – the Land of the Dead: so harsh, so inhospitable seemed the land of Marwar to the Rathores, wandering to this desert from the plains of the Ganges.

The story of the Rathore dynasty materialises from the mists of legend into the light of historical reality in AD 470, when Nayan Pal conquered the kingdom of Kanauj. The Rathores trace their origins to Rama, hero of the epic *Ramayana*, and are therefore Suryavanshis, descendants of the sun. Kanauj reached its pinnacle of glory during the time of Jai Chand in the late 12th century, but dissension among the Rajput clans, in particular enmity with Prithviraj Chauhan, ruler of Delhi, prevented a united stand against the Muslims.

After the defeat of Prithviraj at Tarain in 1192, Muhammad Ghori conquered Kanauj. Jai Chand was drowned in the Ganges; his grandson, Seoji, led his followers under the *pancharanga*, the five-coloured flag of the Rathores, to carve out a new kingdom. Successive generations subdued the Jats and the Bhattis of the Thar, and Rao Chanda in the 15th century overthrew the Parihar ruler of Mandor; thus the Rathores became lords of Marwar.

Rao Chanda had 14 sons and one of them, Rao Raimul, became regent to his own grandson, heir to the Mewar throne at Chitor. Conspiring to win Chitor, Rao Raimul was outwitted and met an ignominious end there: slain, tied to his bed with his own turban by a courtesan. One of his 24 sons, Rao Jodha, was at Chitor and fled, hoping to find refuge at Mandor, but the Chitor nobles were already surrounding it. He

Composite dynastic portraits of the rulers of Marwar.

Jodhpur Fort.

The richly tiered galleries and terraces of the western range of the fort palace.

travelled on several miles through scrub and bush and came upon a hermit on the rocky spur known as Bukerchirria, Bird's Nest, who advised him to abandon Mandor and build a new castle.

Thus in 1459 the foundations of Jodhpur or Meherangarh, as it is called, were laid. Perched high like an eyrie on its rocky outcrop, its eastern towers and bastions stand out like tough sinews, gleaming with a copper tinge where the rock itself was hewn to form the walls and ramparts. From these the view commands the horizon on all sides: indeed, from the Man Mahal may be seen the towers of Khumbhalgarh, 80 miles away to the south.

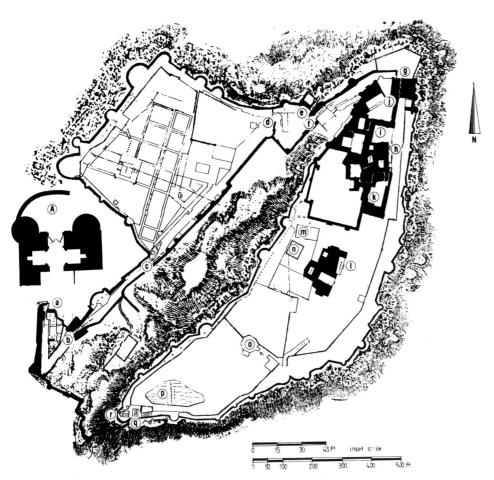

Plan of Jodhpur:
a. Fateh Gate
b. Gopal Gate
c. Bhairon Gate
d. Toati Gate
e. Dodhkangra Gate
f. Amarti Gate
g. Loha Gate
h. Suraj Gate
i. Moti Mahal

j. Phul Mahal
k. Zenana
l. Salim Kot
m. Murli Manoharji Temple
n. Tank
o. Ankaranji Temple
p. Chamunda-ki-Nadi
q. Kalka Temple
r. Chamunda Temple

31 suttee hands in a wall at the entrance to the fort.

The approach climbs steeply from the south, roughly parallel to the western side, then rounds the northern tip to go back along the eastern flank. It is guarded by seven gates, of which the fourth has been destroyed. The first gate, Fateh Pol, between twin bastions, has a curved barbican forcing a 45° turn. The lintel is supported on corbels in the Hindu manner, but the second, third and fifth gates have elegant arches. The sixth gate, Loha Pol, controls the final turn round the northern end, and the seventh, Suraj Pol, leads sideways from the eastern passage into the *durbar* court.

Rao Jodha's 14 sons in turn set out to make their fortunes; there were seven ruling princes among the cadets of the house, including Rao Bhika, founder of Bikaner. Siraj Mah succeeded Rao Jodha in 1491 but fell in time to invading Pathans; Jalore earned its name as a famous Rathore fort during this time. His son, Ganga Singh, joined Rana Sanga of Chitor to fight Babur, and Maldeo, succeeding in his turn, became

61

the most powerful of the Rajput princes after Rana Sanga's death. Embittered by the loss of his son at the battle of Khanua, Maldeo refused aid to Babur's son, Humayun, fleeing from Sher Shah. Twenty years later Akbar, Humayun's son, avenged himself on the Rajputs until even Maldeo sued for peace. He sent his son to the Moghul court, and on succeeding to his father's honours Rao Udai Singh received the title Raja from Akbar in return for a Rathore princess given in marriage.

From that time the Rathore house was bound to the fortunes of the Moghuls, and the once sterile land of Marwar flourished with trade, its palaces gay with colour and ostentation, its courts brilliant with pomp. Raja Sur conquered Gujarat and part of the Deccan for Akbar; Raja Gaj Singh quelled the rebellion of Prince Khurram against his father, the Emperor Jehangir. For this he was awarded the honour of Viceroy of the Deccan, and the Marwar horses thereafter were exempted from branding with the imperial insignia.

Maharaja Jaswant Singh commanded the armies of Shahjahan. Then came a change of fortune: Aurangzeb, prejudiced against Hindus, plotted the murder of Jaswant Singh's son. Heartbroken, the Maharaja died soon afterwards, but a posthumous son, Ajit Singh, survived to expel the Moghul governor from Jodhpur after Emperor Aurangzeb's death. Defeated in 1708 by Bahadur Shah, Ajit Singh again drove the Moghuls from Jodhpur and from Amber, and the Emperor, occupied then by the Sikh war, made peace with the rebel Rajputs. Six queens and 58 concubines of Ajit Singh became *suttees* on his funeral pyre; their palm impressions may be seen on the Loha Pol, the Iron Gate. Though banned by several ordinances since 1829, there have been *suttees* at Jodhpur within the last ten years. All *suttees* carry with them into death the *Gita*, the Hindu holy book; legend has it that the *Gita* will never perish in the flames.

Like all the most spectacular palaces of the Rajputs, constrained by existing fortifications, Jodhpur provides a picturesque contrast between the exigencies of defence and the flamboyance of prosperous peace. Despite typically haphazard extension, it has three reasonably defined areas: the outer, service court – stables, kitchens, shrines for the workforce; the principal court of public audience – the *durbar* hall, reception rooms and the Maharaja's personal apartments; and the sealed *zenana*, with apartments for the royal ladies round a communal Rang Mahal, all surmounted by extensive roof terraces.

Jodhpur's magnificent Meherangarh Museum contains much to delight and absorb the visitor: palanquins, howdahs and ornate cradles, all marvellously preserved and maintained, and many miniatures of the famous Jodhpur school of painting. The Armoury, with its variety of Indian weapons, has no equal. *Kamangars, dhabdars,*

OPPOSITE *The* gadi, *the octagonal golden throne of the Jodhpur rulers for over 300 years and, below, a door panel inlaid with ivory.*

Open kiosks like eyries crown the towering ramparts of the eastern range.

sikligars – bowyers, armourers, swordsmiths – all lived in the fort and were famed both for their skill and their artistry: sword and dagger hilts could be covered in calligraphy or other designs. They made daggers with leaf-shaped, curved, pointed or double-edged blades; swords slender or heavy, curved or straight, for use on horseback or on foot; war axes double-headed or oval-headed or flower-shaped; there are shields of rhino hide, crocodile skin, bamboo, wood or steel; and body armour for man and beast, including the *pakhar* for an elephant's trunk.

Abai Singh led one of the last major campaigns in the Deccan, returning in triumph to Jodhpur with the spoils; his extraordinary campaign tent is also in the Museum. Abai Singh's Phool Mahal, Palace of Flowers, displays the increasingly decorated and opulent style of the

Maharaja Takhat Singh's bedroom decorated with wall paintings of the Jodhpur School.

RIGHT *Durbar-e-Khash, the Hall of Private Audience in Phool Mahal. Portraits of former rulers decorate the lavishly gilded ceiling. The Jodhpur Arms are displayed above the royal couch.*

FAR RIGHT *The campaign tent of Maharaja Abai Singh of Jodhpur, richly embroidered in gold on velvet, was rediscovered recently in the fort and is one of the few remaining in India.*

64

18th century: repeated, inverted forms, all luxuriously exaggerated – cusped arches, domes of lotus petals, *chadyas, chattris*, balconies and *jalis*.

The following century was one of declining fortune, as Marathas, Pathans, Pindaris, neighbouring Rajputs and the British fought over the disintegrating Moghul Empire, though the Rathores lived at Jodhpur till the 1920s. In 1819 one of the last *durbars* was held; the royal *gadi* or throne, given to Jodhpur by Shahjahan, was placed beneath a richly embroidered canopy supported by silver columns. Man Singh had earlier signed the treaty of 'defensive alliance, perpetual friendship, protection and subordinate co-operation' with the East India Company, but still the cry resounded for him in the great reception hall: 'Raj, Raj Iswara – the King, the lord of Kings!'

Anka Ranji Temple, which houses the silver deities of the Rathores of Marwar.

66

Along the ramparts commanding the town, a part of the fort's collection of antique cannon.

Weapons from the Maan Vilas Armory, a part of the Meherangarh Museum.

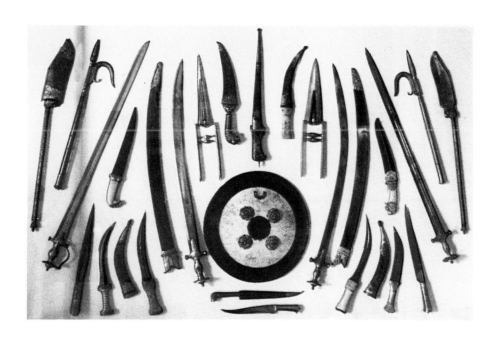

JAISALMER

Paniharis, *water carriers, file before the fort, lending colour to the arid landscape.*

Shifting sands, barren ridges, jutting rocks of sandstone, limestone, flint, reflect for mile upon mile the beating sun in silent, fearsome glare. Eyes seek respite from the aching emptiness – and there, to fill the gaze, beckon the golden walls of Jaisalmer, seeming to sway with liquid grace, like the slow swirl of a Rajasthani skirt, dancing abstracted and alone before the Lord Krishna.

In a scarred, romantic land, Jaisalmer is perhaps the most fascinating discovery for visitors to India, a forgotten, feudal outpost where palaces, *havelis*, temples and bazaars create a magic, mediaeval city of the Orient. At every turn, it seems, there are glimpses of an older, fiercer way of life, a life made hard and vital by its remote and austere setting. Proud, turbanned figures, impassive faces, atop slow, swaying camels; graceful *panharis* walking from the village wells, brass water pots balanced on their heads; the clamour and clangour and colour of bazaars; kohl-rimmed eyes, bangles, ankle bells; a thousand ancient secrets kept, behind the fortress gates, among the streets and alleys of the teeming quarters.

Rawal Jaisal came to the Trikuta, the three-peaked mountain here, from Lodurva, one-time capital of his house. His ancestors had abandoned their old kingdom of Gujarat and moved to lands west of the Indus, thence to the Punjab, under Prince Bhatti. Expelled by the invading Arabs, they were forced into the desert; in the 9th century

70

Deoraj built the fortress of Deogarh, and in the 10th century they took Lodurva from the Pratiharas. Rawal Jaisal's arrival at the Trikuta realised the prophecy, recounted in the *Mahabharata*, that one day a descendant of the moon and Lord Krishna would come to build a capital by the sweet water struck from the rock by the discus of his forefather. Lord Krishna's silver umbrella is said to have been housed for many years in the fortress, where all the furniture was also made of silver, the colour of the ancestral moon.

Jaisalmer became a coveted stronghold on the great trade route from Persia and Afghanistan. The Delhi Sultan, Ala-ud-din Khilji, incensed by the seizure of one of his caravans bringing tribute, laid siege to wreak his vengeance. The Rawal was Jait Singh – his sons had waylaid and pillaged the Sultan's treasure – and he led his garrison of 5000 in their resolute defence while his sons attacked the besiegers from without. The siege lasted eight years, and during this time one of the sons, Rattan Singh, struck up a friendship with Nawab Mahboob Khan, the opposing general. Every day the two would meet to talk and to play chess, until a bugle summoned them to battle. Finally, in 1295, the Rajputs broke, and the Rawal prepared for the *johar*. Rattan Singh's young sons were given into the kind safekeeping of the Nawab, but 24,000 women and children perished as their menfolk rushed upon the enemy.

The double-tiered bastions, still displaying stone cannon balls.

Suraj Pol, the main gate to the fort.

RIGHT *The distinctive filigree work of Jaisalmer's* havelis, *merchants' houses:* ABOVE *Patna Haveli and Dewan-Salim-Singh Haveli;* BELOW *Mathmalji Haveli and detail of an oriel window.*

Jaisalmer was ruined. After two years the Muslims left and the Rathores of Marwar tried to settle there; but by then the Bhatti chiefs had recovered enough to drive them out. Once again they became strong raiders and menaced the desert caravans. They also attacked the bands of pilgrims bound for Mecca. One of their victims was the Begum of Agra: seeing her long, thick plait woven with diamonds, one adventurer struck it off with a single stroke of his sword. Among the treasure also looted was a belt buckle, carved from a single emerald and said to have belonged to Humayun. In one campaign the Bhattis carried off the matchless stud of Sultan Firoz Shah Tughluq from Ajmer. His army pursued them across the Great Thar to Jaisalmer; for the second time within a few decades the *johar* was ordered and the Rawal was killed in the final charge.

The Emperor Akbar determined to reduce the power of the Rajputs and one by one their kingdoms succumbed, including, in 1570, Jaisalmer, ushering in an era not just of peace but of prosperity, as merchants from Iraq, Persia, Arabia and Egypt bartered their goods for silks, spices, indigo and opium. The conquest of northern India by the Delhi Sultans had made Jaisalmer more than just an important trading post; it had become a refuge for Hindu and Jain merchants, bankers and artists. The strength of Jaisalmer was soon matched by its beauty, for the Rawals and the merchants used their wealth to build.

The elegant group of interconnecting Jain temples in the fort, dedicated to Mahavira, Parshvanath, Shantinath and Rishabhanath, date from the early 14th century. Hindus, whose cremation rites allow

The royal memorial chattris *of Jaisalmer ancestors who claim their descent from the moon and Lord Krishna.*

of no burial and therefore no tomb, did build memorial *chattris*; many adorn the tanks of Jaisalmer, revealing later Muslim influences in their prominent oriels and balconies, many-cusped arches, deeply curved roofs and luxurious ornament. Most of the imposing double ring of walls and 99 bastions are early 14th century, though their height was raised in the 16th. The three gates, Suraj, Ganesha and Hawa Pols, were altered then; the outer gate was added in the 18th century, when the city walls were expanded.

In twisting, turning passages lie the *havelis*, residences, of the merchants. Like an exotic flower, the Salim Singh Ki Haveli from its narrow base of a heavy panelled door blooms and blossoms into balconies, domes and spacious pavilions at the top, the receptive sandstone ornately chiselled and carved by Muslim craftsmen to produce exquisite *jali*-work. Sandstone was used as timber might have been, for posts and beams in the traditional Hindu manner, with the *jali*-work inserted into grooves cut in them.

At the highest point within the triangular fort the walls of the old palace rise up from the traditional 'blind' ground floor to balconied main storeys; a beautifully carved gateway leads to the Gadi-sar Tank, filled from rainwater in the monsoon months; and high over it all stands the Megh Darbar, the Cloud Tower, seen like a mirage from the desert and helping to make Jaisalmer one of the unforgettable sights of India.

Desert tribesmen and their camels, the foundation of Jaisalmer's prosperity.

BIKANER

'**O**ut of the silken darkness of a desert dawn emerged the dream of Bikaner.'

For thirty years after leaving his father's capital of Jodhpur, Rao Bhika and his Rathore followers lived from skirmish to skirmish on the edge of life in a hostile land. Gujars, Pratiharas, Chauhans, Afghans, Bhattis and Rajputs fought with one another for supremacy and here, deep in country which had, it seemed, even less to offer than Marwar, Bhika won a kingdom for himself and ruled as 'Lord of the Desert of Bikaner'.

Colonel James Todd wrote early in the 19th century in his *Annals of Rajasthan*, 'The Rathores of Bikaner are unchanged in their martial qualifications, bearing as high a reputation as any other class in India; and whilst their brethren of Marwar, Amber, and Mewar have been for years groaning under the rapacious visitations of Mahrattas and Pathans, their distance and the difficulties of the country have saved them from such afflictions: though, in truth, they have had enough to endure at home, in the tyranny of their own lord. The Rathores of the desert have fewer prejudices than their more eastern brethren; they will eat food, without enquiring by whom it was dressed, and will drink either wine or water, without asking to whom the cup belonged. They would make the best soldiers in the world if they would submit to discipline, as they are brave, hardy, easily satisfied, and very patient; though, on the other hand, they have imbibed some qualities, since their migration to these regions, which could only be eradicated in the

Early suttee *hands at the entrance of Bikaner's Junagarh, with palace and court façade.*

Ganga Niwas Palace inside the fort walls.

rising generation: especially the inordinate use of opium, and smoking intoxicating herbs, in both which accomplishments "the sons of Beeka" are said to bear the palm from the rest of the *Chatees rajcúla*, the thirty-six royal tribes of India. The *pialá*, or "cup", is a favourite with every Rajpoot who can afford it, and is, as well as opium, a panacea for *ennui*, arising from the absence of all mental stimulants, in which they are more deficient, from the nature of the country, than most of their warlike countrymen.'

It was during the reign of Rao Rai Singh, sixth in line from Rao Bhika, that Junagarh was built. Its main entrance is through the huge, arched Suraj Pol; on the walls nearby may be seen two groups of *suttee* hands, mute testimony to battles fought and lost. But by the 16th century such desperate days were in the past and the creamy palace walls overtopped their defensive brethren with lofty unconcern. Rao Rai Singh had made peace with Akbar and become one of his most distinguished generals; consequently Bikaner lay in safety while its rulers fought elsewhere, like Anup Singh in the 17th century, who campaigned from the Deccan to Kabul for Aurangzeb. The princes of Bikaner often brought back artists from these far-off regions, introducing Moghul style to their palaces and their adornment, and laying the foundations of the famous Bikaner school of painting.

Bikaner is undoubtedly one of the most artistic, interesting, best

The 19th-century wing of the palace reveals mixed European and traditional Rajput influences.

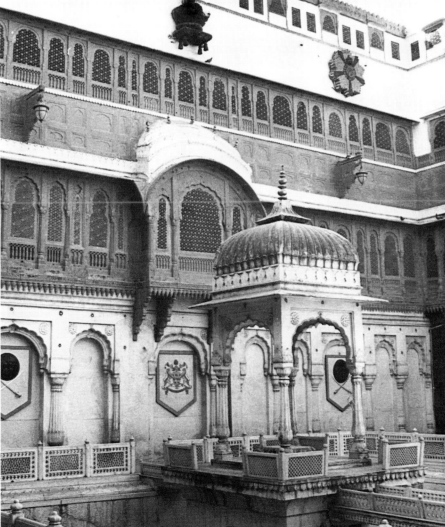

Swords upon which fakhirs *formerly danced.*

A moated throne platform below the royal insignia in the durbar *court.*

preserved and well maintained forts in India, and its museum is deservedly renowned. Each of the palaces contains particular treasures, like the famous *hindola* or swing, in the Anup Mahal, one of the few perfect specimens left. One courtyard is set with tiles to look like a carpet and it was here that *fakhirs* used to dance upon swords, their sharp blades upturned. The Karni Museum contains collections of Bikaner miniatures, *shikar* trophies and a very good armoury full of historical Indian weapons and European guns.

Raja Gaj Singh in the mid-18th century unintentionally created problems for Bikaner's future: producing 61 children in an otherwise uneventful reign, he ensured horrific disputes over the succession. But he also gained a measure of immortality by building a wing of beautiful palaces. The Chandra Mahal, or Moon Palace, and the Phool Mahal, Palace of Flowers, date from his time, the latter decorated with motifs of flowers and delicately inlaid with mirrorwork. The Phool Mahal contains a bed reputed to have belonged to Rao Bhika himself. Its small size is explained by a curious story: his grandfather had been killed tied helpless to his bed; mindful of this, Rao Bhika always used a bed a good deal too short, so that if a similar fate ever overtook him he would be able to stand, bed and all, to give battle.

Murder, poisoning and intrigue followed Gaj Singh's death and eventually Surat Singh took control. His warlike temperament involved Bikaner in many battles, not least in the succession disputes of Jodhpur. But during his reign the elegant Anup Mahal rose to grace Bikaner with its beautifully sculpted red sandstone walls and magnificent rooms decorated with designs of trees, flowers, clouds and figures. The lovely Ganga Niwas audience hall was added in the 19th century.

Like earlier forces, the famous Bikaner Camel Corps fought far from home and the Bikaner princes maintained a distinguished presence in European affairs from the First World War onwards. They lived in the fort until the 1920s when Maharaja Ganga Singh, who had come to the throne in 1887 at the age of seven, built Lalgarh, the red fort. It combined many Renaissance techniques with Rajput traditions, but it was built outside the fortress walls, explicitly leaving behind any pretence at fortification. Set in wonderful gardens, it houses today the celebrated Anup Sanskrit Library.

In Junagarh it is easy to imagine exactly what life in a fort was like, as everything has been left in place. At the very top of the fort, built on the roof of one palace, is a single room, its white ceiling shaped like the roof of a tent and painted in red and gold with flowers, leaves and a frieze of graceful dancing Rajput ladies. From the ceiling a heavy, embroidered *punka* hangs and sways over a low bed on silver feet. This was the favourite room of the Maharaja, open to the desert breeze on all sides and somehow embodying in its delicate beauty the whole of Bikaner's extraordinary artistic flowering in the midst of desolation.

The great warriors, Jaimal and Patta, mounted on elephants, are guardians of Suraj Pol.

Three of the five Elephant Gates inside the fort.

81

Fine sandstone columns support elephant brackets of a palace portico.

Lavish interiors of Anup Mahal within the fort: decorative lightning rends vivid blue stormclouds in one of the ante-chambers; the richness of a Moghul carpet is reflected in the gilt ceiling of another; the mirror-encrusted gold canopy over the royal couch in the Hall of Private Audience; and the famous Bikaner swing.

AMBER

An elephant waits to carry travellers up the steep ascent to Amber Fort.

84

In a setting of wild, romantic beauty, Amber seems like a phantom of the *Arabian Nights*, a mysterious enchantment of glistening turrets and 'cloud-capp'd towers' above tranquil waters, which, after Delhi and Agra, lures more visitors than any other place in northern India.

A succession of fortified Aravalli hills stand guard over the approaches to Amber, chief amongst them Narwargarh, the Tiger Fort, and culminating in the formidable Jaigarh, high on the hill overlooking the palaces in their rocky mountain gorge. Jaiwaan, the great cannon of Jaigarh, was the largest in all Asia, made in the famous foundry there. Its purpose was not just to protect the resplendent palaces: Jaigarh itself housed the fabled treasures of the Kachhwaha rulers, amassed during their campaigns on the frontiers of the empire.

Amber had belonged to the Mina tribe and took its name from their goddess, Amba Mata, Mother Earth. The Minas gave shelter to a Kachhwaha queen, exiled with her young son Dhola Rao, heir to the throne of Narwar and descended from Kush, son of the immortal hero Rama. The Minas were skilled archers adept at mountain warfare and they taught the young Kachhwaha prince all they knew. In 1150 Dhola Rao repaid his benefactors by wresting Amber from them and holding them as hereditary servitors to guard the Kachhwahas and their treasures. Shiva became the presiding deity, worshipped as Ambikeshwara.

The court of the Sukh Nivas, the private apartments of Maharaja Jai Singh. The gardens were for ceremonial court purposes and for courtships.

Visitors gaze down on an expansive view from the Jai Mandir, celebrated in all Rajasthan for its translucent glass mosaics.

Ganesha Pol and a detail of inlaid mirror work recessed for lighted candles within the private apartments.

Two of the most celebrated rulers of Amber were Man Singh and his great-nephew Jai Singh. In 1555 Raha Bihar Mal, who had earlier acknowledged the suzerainty of Babur and Humayun, gained the trust of Akbar. His daughter was the Rajput princess for whom Akbar built Fatehpur Sikri, and Bihar Mal also gave into Akbar's service his adopted grandson, Man Singh, whose integrity and martial skills made him legendary.

Akbar's enlightened religious tolerance and the Rajput's loyalty ensured long years of affluence and concord. Man Singh was a patron of all the arts; architecture, sculpture, painting, all flourished at his court in happy union of Hindu and Muslim styles. He built his palace in about 1580 and began the beautiful Kali Temple, the family shrine at Amber, which also dates from this time, its pillars and capitals carved into marvellous plantain and banana trees in delicate shades of green marble. It is dedicated to Shila Mata, a meteorite deity brought back by Man Singh from Jessore in Bengal, and even today the head *pujari* is a Bengali. Kali was deified by the martial Rajputs as goddess of war and worshipped by the *thags* and brigands who once roamed at large in Rajputana.

The distinguished Jai Singh, otherwise known as the Mirza Raja, contributed even more to the glories of Amber. His Diwan-i-Am, Hall of Public Audience, is a marvel to behold. A double row of delicately carved columns, sandstone then marble, with elephant capitals, supports a vaulted canopy below a galleried terrace with far-reaching views. The hall's reputed magnificence provoked the envy of the Emperor Jehangir, who sent his commissioners to examine and if necessary raze it to the ground to humble its creator. Hastily, Jai Singh had the columns covered with stucco, but where time has eroded this the exquisite workmanship beneath is visible. On the south side of Jai Singh's majestic *baradari* is the ceremonial Ganesha Pol, covered with mosaics and sculptures with beautiful marble lattice windows above, leading to a garden court with the Sukh Nivas, the Hall of Pleasure, to the right.

Though Hindu buildings might be set in landscapes of great scenic beauty, the formal garden is a specifically Muslim addition to India's palaces and temples which had its origin in Persia. To India's invading Muslim desert-dwellers, a garden was a place of luxury, the original Eden of Sumer, the Bagh-i-Wafa. The lake garden at Amber, viewed from the *zenana* windows, seems indeed a floating Paradise, crisscrossed with flowerbeds and pathways like a fallen galaxy of stars.

To one side is the Jai Mandir, containing the Shish Mahal, the Hall of Mirrors, and the Diwan-i-Khas. A single flame in the dim interior of the Shish Mahal creates a myriad dancing reflections, a breathtaking and somehow unexpected effect. Surrounded by a verandah with cusped arches, the walls of the Diwan-i-Khas are painted with delicate murals — flowers and leafy scrolls, with designs of lamps and goblets interspersed, in a kaleidoscope of green and turquoise. The doors are of sandalwood inlaid with ivory. The storey above has the alabaster Jas Mahal; from its latticed windows there are stunning views over the garden, lake and mountains.

In 1699 Jai Singh II succeeded, a man remembered as an outstanding statesman and administrator, for the five observatories he built and for the founding, in 1728, of a new capital at Jaipur. Court life at Amber was gradually abandoned; the glorious palaces, within their seven gates, were shrouded in the silence of absence and departure. Now elephants, impressively caparisoned, bring visitors to Amber in the time-honoured way: life and bustle and laughter have returned.

Serpentine crenellations at Nilahgarh. Many such forts stood sentinel over the Kachhwaha realm.

Jaiwaan, the gigantic cannon of Jaigarh, is the largest in all Asia.

89

RANTHAMBHOR

Ranthambhor stands on an isolated rocky plateau, its haunted ruins half-concealed amongst thick jungle and dead silver trees. The forests that had been some of India's finest tiger shooting country have become the Swai Madhopur game reserve. Wild animals make their home in the ghostly palaces and empty barracks: a temple gives sanctuary to monkeys, a mosque to bats, and the tomb of a Muslim saint is watched over by kites.

Only Chitorgarh has a more ancient history than Ranthambhor. Govinda, son of the Chauhan emperor, took this place, a perfect example of a *vana durg* or forest fort, from a branch of the Jadon Rajputs in

The great forest fort of Ranthambhor, surrounded by the area of Swai Madhopur, now a game sanctuary.

1192 after the Chauhan capital, Ajmer, had been sacked; and the fort reached its peak of fame during the reign of the powerful Rao Hamir Derv, who held it strongly till 1301. The codes of conduct in Rajasthan are 'bound by honour and sealed in blood' – not least in Ranthambhor. In that year of 1301 the Chauhans once more defended the fort against the army of Ala-ud-din Khilji, and successfully beat off the first assault, killing the Sultan's general with a catapult. Ala-ud-din then marched to take charge of the siege himself; it lasted a year and ended in *johar* for the Rajputs, victory for the Muslims.

In 1516 the Malwa chiefs seized Ranthambhor but in 1528 the Sisodia Rana Sanga made the fort over to Babur. Babur died in 1530 and amid the turmoil of Humayun's first reign and that of Sher Shah, Ranthambhor achieved again a measure of independence. However, in 1569 the Moghuls wrested it back. The site which had made Ranthambhor so inaccessible in the past now made it vulnerable: from the surrounding hills, the Emperor Akbar's artillery devastated the fort, its palaces and temples for 37 days. Eventually he brought about its defeat by bribing the Bundi defender, Surjana Hara. Despite continuing stout resistance by other Rajputs, Ranthambhor fell.

The fort's mostly 13th-century crenellated walls and bastions rise sheer; access to them is by the north-east face of Ranthambhor's crag, 700 feet above the plain, the ascent so steep that steps have been hewn from the rock. Overhanging cliffs, jagged rocks, dense forest, form natural obstacles to which Ranthambhor's rulers added their own. Four gates bar the twisting path. Once past the heavily chained, massive,

The ghostly remains of temples and palaces tower above the ramparts.

91

One of the fort's forgotten temples, now the sanctuary of monkeys.

RIGHT *A* chattri *commemorates Ranthambhor's chivalrous past.*

BELOW LEFT *The fourth and final gate of the tortuous ascent to the fort.*

A suttee *stone in the wall of the fort and, below, the enigmatic monolith of Ranthambhor.*

spiked door, the barbican of the first forces three right-angled turns, a defensive manoeuvre repeated in the second gate. The third is placed after a sharp turn to foil the use of a battering ram and the fourth, though so far up, is heavily spiked. Outside the third gate stands a monolithic head, dating from very ancient times, over six feet high and enigmatic as a sphinx.

Ranthambhor passed into the hands of the Jaipur rulers towards the end of the 17th century. Gradually they had less need of a martial fortress-palace, preferring the softer splendours of Amber and their later new capital at Jaipur. Spirits of the chivalric past were left to rule the ruins and Ranthambhor was left to its slow, leafy metamorphosis.

BUNDI

The black log crashed above the white;
The little flames and lean,
Red as slaughter and blue as steel,
That whistled and fluttered from head to heel,
Leaped up anew, for they found their meal
On the heart of – The Boondi Queen!

From 'The Last Suttee'
written at Bundi in 1889
RUDYARD KIPLING

Startling upon its hilltop stands Taragarh, the Star Fort, where the Hara kings first came to glory and held sway. For almost 600 years Taragarh has been spoken of as a treasury of untold riches, guarded down the ages by Pathans who came campaigning from Kabul and stayed in loyal service.

Bundi was founded in 1342 by Rao Deva Hara of the Hara Chauhan clan. After their defeat by Mohammad Ghori in 1192, the Chauhans had taken refuge in Chitorgarh and remained the Rana of Mewar's staunch allies. Seeking independence, however, Deva Hara and his followers struck out to find a stronghold of their own. In land claimed by Chitor, they fought and conquered the Bhil and Mina tribes of the rocky Chambal valley and called their tiny kingdom Daravati. The river at Bando Nala was made their boundary and here the Haras built their city, along the *bund* or embankment.

Every Rajasthani fortress has its share of myth and legend and one of Bundi's most famous tales concerns a prophecy of centuries ago. Then it was foretold that if a prince of Bundi and a Rana of Udaipur should meet, the death of one of them would result. Four times in 300 years a prince of each house met, and four times one of them died at the hands of the other.

Within its crenellated walls, the rocky acres of Taragarh are dominated by a large tower, Bhim Burj, which used to house one of the most famous cannon in this region, the 16th-century Garbh-Ganjam, now lost but similar to the cannon at Bijapur and Armadnagar, and cast in the same period. The artilleryman who lit the cannon's fuse had to jump into a deep well to save his eardrums. Men say that there is as much room

The hill fort of Taragarh, Star Fort, dominates the Chatar Mahal and the town of Bundi.

Bhim Burj and its ramp built for the famous cannon, Garbh-Ganjam.

beneath the ground at Taragarh as there is above, subterranean chambers linked by passages to the Chatar Mahal, to the town below and to the neighbouring hills, so that Bundi's defenders could escape and live to fight another day.

The history of the Hara clan is written in two books, *Vansh Bhaskar* and *Prarara Hadi Rao*, both in possession of the Bundi family. Under Akbar, Surjana Hara accepted Moghul overlordship in return for religious freedom and imperial honours: Rao Chatar Sal was made Governor of Delhi by Shahjahan, a rare privilege for a Rajput. In the Moghul wars of succession the head of every Hara clan and 12 Hara princes died in the battles to decide which of the Moghul princes would rule Hindusthan. Chatar Sal himself had died fighting at Samugarh, charging in the famous Hara formation known as *gole*, a circular mass of men bristling with lances, sabres and spears – valorous but no match for artillery. In the years that followed, Bundi's disputes were among neighbouring Rajputs, and the kingdom retreated from the rush and clamour of imperial history.

As the strength of the Haras was proved, they had moved down from their hilltop to build outside the fortress walls. The Chatar Mahal dates from 1660, built from local serpentine stone. Each palace is the legacy of a different Raja, but the pavilions, turrets, colonnades and balconies of each are all in predominantly Rajput style, so that Bundi unfurls in harmonious theme and variation along the hillside.

Tradition has it that each ruler of Bundi was permitted but once, on his accession, to see its fabled treasure and choose one thing for himself; led blindfold among the twisting caverns, he would never be able to find the hoard again. The cache was last seen at the turn of this century. During the Second World War the faithful old Pathan who knew the secret of its whereabouts died. On his return from the Burma Front, the late Maharaja Bahadur Singh tried hard to excavate the fort, but, unfortunately, the discovery of treasure was not written in his horoscope.

All through Bundi runs a sense of past romance and brave *suttee* queens, of valour and of chivalry: the Rani Mahal at Taragarh, standing reflected in a large tank, with delicate, fading miniatures on walls and coloured glass in windows; the arsenal where gunpowder for Garbh-Ganjam was made; a small Shiva mandir. All palaces in India, even the dead ones, are full of eyes. In some the feeling of being watched is stronger than others; in Bundi it is overpowering. In one deserted pavilion, it is said a Bundi queen was walled up alive in dreadful retribution for some supposed wrongdoing.

One road down to the town runs past the Chatar Mahal and two great gates: Hathi Pol, where huge stone elephants form an arch, and Hazari Pol, Gate of a Thousand, where the garrison was housed. The other route is by the spiked Ganesha Pol down a stony path on a steep incline through thorny jungle. It makes for a rough jeep ride but affords quite a different perspective on Bundi's *trompe l'oeuil* castellations.

Viewed from the town, a medieval confusion of narrow streets and piling roof tops that has hardly changed since the 14th century, the palaces of Bundi look like a cascade of stone, petrified in a moment of time from an heroic past.

A view from above the ramparts showing a distant watchtower.

The Rani's Palace reflected in the waters of one of Bundi's many tanks.

KISHANGARH

'Astar-scattered sky whose reflections dance upon the lake like
diamond water lilies, where silence prevails save for the sound
of crickets and the echo of leaping fish.'

Kishangarh never was a place for battles and sieges, intrigues and
treacheries. Founded in 1597 by Kishan Singh, a Rathore prince, son
of Raja Udai Singh of Jodhpur, the tiny principality was tightly hemmed
in by the kingdoms of Mewar, Amber and Marwar – in fact for many
years it had been part of Marwar. Kishangarh's greatness lay in its
artists and their exquisite paintings.

Reflected in the limpid waters of Lake Gandalan, Kishangarh is
undeniably picturesque: brave battlements; courtyards of rambling
zenanas, more like secret gardens now; steep steps up to creaking
wooden doors lead to shady balconies with *purdah* screens, from

The Elephant Gate of Kishangarh with its painted guardians.

where the ruler's ladies could espy the court unseen. Brightly coloured panes of glass in windows and in doors trace their glow along white-washed walls, the only movement now among these empty, dusty chambers.

Kishangarh was too small to support all its princes, who would generally disport themselves at the imperial court in Delhi, breaking off their amusements, nonetheless, when it became necessary to fight the foe – which they did valiantly and well, as far afield as Afghanistan. But after the Moghuls, Kishangarh accepted British protection and suzerainty and, sheltered from the strife besetting its more important neighbours, devoted its energies to art.

In the fort's temple there are beautiful miniatures of religious epics and deities behind locked, heavy silver doors; but it is among the straggling palaces that the full glory of the paintings is revealed.

Elephants escort the visitor here – in attendance at the entrances, along the walls of the durbar court, supporting the lotus baths. A charming story exists about the inspiration for many of the court paintings. Sawant Singh, seventh in line after Kishan Singh, abdicated his throne in 1757 after only nine years' reign: a poet-mystic, he decided to leave ceremonial life to worship Krishna at Brindaban. His poems, using the pseudonym Nagri Das, had throbbed with love and passion and romantic fervour, penned in praise of a beautiful courtesan, Bani Thani, with whom he had fallen in love. Nihal Chand, a Brahman, was court painter and worked some masterpieces to illustrate the verses; the likenesses of Bani Thani became the apogee of allure – tapering waists; long, curved eyes, dark like forest water; a languid grace; vital colours in a desert oasis.

Of the fort, much has fallen to time and weather; but from the battlements the views are unchanged, like a Kishangarh painting brought to life, all green and blue, with arbours and slender kiosks mirrored in the lake: only the royal lovers are missing.

The durbar *court of the fort palace.*

100

The external audience platform
beneath the Umbrella of State.

BELOW *Brass antique temple doors
with paintings from the Kishangarh
School.*

101

GAUR

The earth ramparts of Gaur.

BELOW *Dakhil Gate constructed of finely-coursed red brick.*

Gaur, near Malda in West Bengal, is one of India's rare surviving examples of a *mahi durg*, or mud fort. Built near the confluence of the Ganges from the west and the Mahananda from the east, the entire site covers many square miles, while the citadel itself stretches one mile from north to south. The ramparts on the three river and swamp sides are massive enough, more as protection from flooding; but the remains of the northern approach earthworks are impressive indeed – they were six miles wide, consisting of two or even three great ditches and ramparts of colossal proportions – 30 feet high and 180 feet thick at the base.

Gaur emerges in history as the capital of one of the many independent kingdoms formed from the ruins of the Gupta Empire. Harsha Vardana in the 7th century became overlord to its king Sasanka, and on Sasanka's death the kingdom was divided into four. A period of confusion followed, eventually ended by the emergence in the 8th century of India's last Buddhist dynasty, the Palas. They were succeeded by the Hindu Senas, originally Brahmans in the Deccan who became Chattriyas when they became soldiers; the Sena scholar-king, Vallal, reorganised the caste system by introducing the theory of caste mobility. The last Sena king, Lakshmana, founded a new city, calling it Lakshmanavati or Lakhnavti.

Bengal was rich land – Gaur took its name from *gur*, the sugar cane cultivated in the area, as it is again today. Around 1200, Muhammad Bakhtiyar Khilji took Gaur in the name of Muhammad Ghori, conqueror of the Hindu Empire and now Sultan of Delhi. For over 100

years there followed gruesome hostilities between the Sultans and the governors of Gaur for control over Bengal, until independence was won from the declining Tughluqs by Ilyas Shah in 1339.

In 1338 Fakhr-ud-din had broken away to found a new Afghan kingdom not far off in Pandua but Gaur again became the undisputed capital of Bengal in 1420. In between times it had endured a succession of regicides, fratricides, and eunuch and harem intrigues: *Takht* or *Takhta* – Throne or Death was the narrow choice. Then the Ilyas Shahi dynasty was ousted in 1396 by the Hindu king Ganesha. His son was obliged by him to convert to Islam to avoid an invasion by the Muslim Jaunpur king, but was forcibly purified again by the Brahmans when the danger had passed. On Ganesha's death his son, still Muslim at heart, persecuted the Hindus thoroughly; there were mass conversions to Islam. Ganesha's grandson was assassinated and the Ilyas Shahis returned in 1442.

Of the Muslim kings of Bengal, the elected Husain Shah was the best loved, by his own and by Hindus. From his accession in 1493 to 1532, the end of his son Nasrat Shah's elected reign, was a time of relative peace and many of the buildings still to be seen at Gaur date from that period. Unluckily, the traditional Bengali building materials – brick and bamboo – are not long-lasting; flooding, erosion and silting by the two rivers have also destroyed much. Still, Husain Shah and Nasrat Shah are not only remembered as builders but as general patrons of the arts, appreciative of Hindu work, too. There existed by about 1390 a Bengali translation of the *Ramayana* and Nasrat Shah ordered a Bengali

Kadam Rasul Mosque.

version of the *Mahabharata* to be written. Nasrat Shah successfully made peace terms with Babur; but in 1537, with Mahmud Shah on the throne, Humayun occupied Gaur – called at this period Jannatabad or Terrestrial Paradise – during his struggle to retain the empire until he was vanquished by Sher Shah. He sacked Gaur, departing with its treasures. Akbar captured Gaur in 1576, but the year before it had been virtually unpeopled by the plague.

The citadel at Gaur dates from the 14th century. The northern entrance is marked by the great gate Dakhil Darwaza, erected in 1465 by Barbak Shah. Once over 100 feet long, it was built of beautifully coursed brick and embossed brickwork. To the west of it may be seen the Golden or Baradwari Mosque, built in 1426 by Nasrat Shah. Of its original 44 gilded domes only one remains, but the six remaining columns, brown stone faced with black marble and carved with flowers, give an impression of its earlier grandeur.

To the east, where there is also another great gate, one building dominates the citadel, the Firoz Shah Minar, built about 1500; there is also a 15th-century tower, Chiragh Minar or Lamp Tower, twelve-sided and turquoise-glazed. The Lattan Masjid or Painted Mosque, probably built about 1475, formerly glowed with enamelled brick in bands of green, yellow, blue and white; the brick of the Tantipara Masjid is embossed, in the manner of Bengal. Nearby is the Piasbari Tank. The name means House of Thirst: reputedly, condemned prisoners were allowed only to drink of its impure water.

The palace was further south, near two more buildings from about 1530 – the tomb of Fateh Shah and the Kadam Rasul, a small mosque built by Nasrat Shah; in it is preserved a stone said to bear the footprint of the Prophet. In the south wall of the city is another gate, Kotwali Darwaza; two miles further south is the Lesser Golden Mosque, dating from about 1600, with fine stone-carved panels.

Further away at Pandua are two 17th-century shrines, a small Golden Mosque with granite walls and ten brick domes, and the Adina Masjid, built by Shikandar Shah about 1360; it was widely reckoned to be the most remarkable building in Bengal, once a glory of pillars and domes, its stone-carved *qibla* and *mimbar* of exquisite workmanship. The ruins of the palace lie hidden nearby in the dense jungle.

Gaur was 'rediscovered' two hundred years ago when Sir William Jones along with his wife, Anna Maria, travelled up the Ganges by way of the ancient city. 'The jungles echoed to the leopard and the great Bengal tiger, pythons lay concealed in the thorn and bamboo, and in the crocodile infested swamps the mosquitoes hummed their own metered drone.' Undaunted by the possibility of a ducking in the river, after a piggyback ride on the wiry and weather-beaten boatmen, the wonderstruck couple stood face to face with the palaces and tombs of Gaur, the remains of successive dynasties over a thousand years. It stands today a unique embodiment of the ancient Hindu *shastras*.

RIGHT *Firoz Shah Minar.*

BELOW *The tomb of Fateh Shah with its* bangaldar *roof.*

JAMMU & KASHMIR

One of nature's most fortunate creations, the Valley of Kashmir has enraptured all who venture there with its beauty. It is an oval plain, some 80 or more miles long and 20 to 25 miles wide, at a height of 5000 feet, set within high mountain ranges. At every turn, in every light, the loveliness of Kashmir is made manifest: floating gardens on the Dal Lake; roses, narcissus and jasmine growing wild; blue pines, deodar, spruce, horse chestnut, cedar, willow and *chenar*, the plane trees that are a special glory of the valley; blossoms of apricot, cherry, peach and mulberry; rivers, brooks and waterfalls; and all around the snow-clad, luminous peaks.

Ancient Kashmir had been a Buddhist land, distinguished for its learning; one of its first kings was the 4th-century scholar Kumanajiva, who took Buddhism to Tibet and was known in China. In the late 6th century Pravarasena founded Srinagar; in the 8th century, when Lalitaditya conquered Kanauj, there were reckoned to be 300 Buddhist monasteries in the region.

For many centuries Kashmir was ruled by Scythian Hindu princes and then by Tartars; but in 1346 Shah Mir, a Muslim in the service of the Hindu Raja, took control of the land. Muslim and Hindu lived peaceably together – Sanskrit remained the official language, the kings took Hindu wives and bestowed lands on the Brahmans – until the Hindu minister of the sixth Sultan, Sikandar, adopted Islam and prohibited his former religion: conversion by the sword, or exile. This painful history ended with the long reign of the eighth Sultan, Zain-ul-Abdin, a man of universal tolerance who encouraged literature, painting, music and who built bridges and irrigation works.

In the late 16th century, Akbar's armies imposed his overlordship on Kashmir; but Akbar desired to possess the valley and sent a second expedition in 1586 that took the land, generally without force of arms, in a *coup d'état*. Akbar built the great imperial route which opened up the Happy Valley to one of the most prosperous periods in its history; but before that came the fort.

The hill at Hari Parbat had long been regarded as a place of great sanctity. Legend told of a water demon, Jalodbhava, who dwelt in the depths of a huge lake. Invincible, he spread ruination among the people till the gods called on Sati Mata for her aid. She took on the form of a little bird and dropped a pebble on the demon. The pebble grew and grew as it fell and crushed the demon to death. Hari Parbat is revered as that pebble and the grateful gods took up residence there. Stones found on the hill are held to represent the 33 *crore* (330 million) gods of the Hindu pantheon.

The ramparts, three miles round, are made from local grey limestone and entered by the domed Kathi Darwaza, decorated with arched panels and medallions; a lesser gate, Sangin Darwaza, is adorned with oriel

The hill fort of Hari Parbat seen from the Dal Lake at Srinagar.

'The Rope Bridge at Srinagar',
aquatint by Thomas Daniell.

windows. It is a simple building, though using stone rather than the more usual carved Kashmiri cedarwood, but an inscription in one of the walls proclaims the greatness of its builder: 'The foundation of the fort was laid in the reign of the just sovereign, the King of Kings, Akbar, unparalleled among the kings of the world, past or future. He sent one *crore* and ten *lakhs* from his treasury and two hundred Indian master-builders, all his servants. No one was forced to work without remuneration. All obtained their wages from his treasury.' In fact the work was commenced hurriedly to provide relief from a dreadful famine that gripped Kashmir and all Hindustan from 1595 for three years.

All the Moghul Emperors loved Kashmir and some left permanent memorials to their time here. Akbar also created the ten, fountained terraces of Nishat Bagh by the Dal Lake; Jehangir made Shalimar Bagh, where he lived in the summer months with Nurjahan, 'the Light of the World'; Shahjahan laid out below the vineyards the cascades, fountains and tanks of the Chasma Shahi. Of the buildings, among the most notable is a beautiful mosque built by Shahjahan's eldest son, Dara Shikoh. Two other mosques in Kashmiri style of carved woodwork

with brick in-filling are the 17th-century Shah Hamadan Masjid and the Jami Masjid, with immense deodar pillars, 50 feet high, turned from whole trees.

With the decline of the Moghul Empire in the 18th century, Kashmir in 1739 was annexed by the Persian Nadir Shah, and in 1748 passed into the hands of the Afghan Ahmad Shah Abdali. In 1819 the Sikhs, under Ranjit Singh, took possession. After the reverses of the first Anglo-Sikh war in 1846 an indemnity of half a million pounds was imposed on the Sikhs. Gulab Singh, the Dogra chief of Jammu, whose people had kept free both from Islam and the Sikh movement, mediated and when the Sikhs failed to pay, he paid double; thus Jammu and Kashmir were conjoined.

A fine view of Srinagar may be had from a hill once named the Takht-i-Sulaiman, the Throne of Solomon, but now called after a Hindu sage of the 8th century, Shankar Acharya, whose stone temple is there. Ancient tombstones elsewhere, charitably inscribed in Sanskrit and in Arabic, bequeath eloquent testament of a past spirit that could transcend, like the sublime heights all around, the puny nature of man.

109

THE SIKH FORT
OF PATIALA

The Sikhs began their concerted opposition to Muslim oppression as guerrilla fighters in the hills and plains of the Punjab, and to begin with had no need of forts. Their battle cry *'Bareh sonehal!'* struck fear into the hearts of all who opposed them: 'They go about heavily armed, frequently bearing a drawn sword in each hand, two other swords in their belt, a matchlock on their back, and on their turbans iron quoits six or eight inches in diameter, with their outer edges sharpened; and these, it is asserted, they throw with such force, as well as precision of aim, as to lop off the leg of a horse.'

It was the tenth and last guru, Gobind Singh, who really founded Sikh military power. Initiates were commanded to wear 'the five K's': *kesh*, unshorn hair and beard; *kuchcha*, short breeches; *kara*, an iron bangle on the right wrist; *kungha*, a comb worn in the hair; and *kirpan*, a small steel dagger. Gobind decided, nonetheless, to support Bahadur Shah in his fight for the throne but Gobind's successor, Banda Singh, was projected as his reincarnation charged with the destruction of the Moghul Empire. He went on the rampage in Sirhind with 40,000 armed Sikhs. Bahadur Shah and then Abdul Samad Khan defeated them; the Sikhs were driven to the hills and hunted down, only coming to a position of strength, in the Punjab at least, on the accession of the Persian Nadir Shah later in the 18th century.

The Sikh movement had been established in the Punjab in the 15th and 16th centuries by the guru Nanak; his Sikhs, or disciples, laid stress on the unity of God, the futility of forms of worship and the unreality of castes. In 1577 Akbar granted to them the tank and Golden Temple at Amritsar, which became the focus of the Sikh faith. Hargobind, the sixth guru, began the change from a sect of pious ascetics to a military brotherhood. Both Jehangir and Shahjahan forced him into retreat in the hill country and Aurangzeb intensified the attacks, appointing temple breakers and executing the ninth guru, Tegh Bahadur.

After the death of Gobind Singh, political power had passed to the whole Sikh community of *Khalsa* and sole spiritual authority was vested in their scriptures, the *Granth Sahib*. The Sikhs, predominantly Jat by race, organised themselves into twelve *misls* or martial brotherhoods, who parcelled out the Punjab between them. Two of the most prominent groups were the 'Sukerchakias' in the Gujranwala and the 'Phulkias' in Jind, Nabha and Patiala. The Patiala chiefs founded a state in the 1760s and Ahmad Shah Abdali, the Afghan ruler who had followed Nadir Shah, conferred the title Raja on Ala Singh.

Ala Singh's headquarters was the great concentric fort at Patiala, the very model of a sophisticated *nara durg*, a fort on the plain, protected by men and strong enough to repulse a fierce Maratha attack in 1794. A stark and commanding moated gun emplacement, Patiala has no softer side: there are no palatial apartments or pleasure gardens here.

The great concentric fort of Patiala.

111

GWALIOR

The ancient hill fort of Gwalior, directly on the main north–south route through the sub-continent, is the key to control of central India. Its strategic significance could never be overlooked by any ambitious potentate, and it has survived so many centuries of strife and struggle for power that it may properly be regarded as a microcosm of the nation's history.

One inscription in the fort records that during the 5th-century reign of Mihiragula the Hun, a temple of the sun was erected here. Later inscriptions reveal that Gwalior was in the kingdom of Kanauj in about 900 under the Gujara Pratihara, King Mihira Bhoja, and that 50 years later the Kachhwaha dynasty had taken it over; they kept Gwalior for nearly 200 years.

The Kachhwahas were the Pal kings of bardic chronicles. According to them, Gwalior was founded in the 4th century by Suraj Sen: hunting on Gopagiri Hill, he was given water to drink by a hermit, Gwalipa, which magically cured him of his leprosy. The hermit pronounced that as long as they kept the name Pal, the line of Suraj Sen would reign at Gwalior. He took the name of Suhan Pal and 83 of his successors held the kingdom, until Tej Karan broke the prohibition. Seven Parihara princes, the first of them his nephew, ruled after him but in 1196 Qutb-ud-bin-Aibak, founder in 1206 of the Delhi slave dynasty, took the fort and held it for 15 years. In 1232 the second Sultan, Iltutmish, recaptured Gwalior.

After the invasion of Timur in 1398, the Tomar chief, Bir Singh Deo, declared independence at Gwalior. Situated less than 200 miles from Delhi, this was perhaps an ambitious move – by the 15th century Gwalior was again paying tribute to Delhi but in the 16th century prolonged hostilities ended in actual surrender to Sultan Ibraham Lodi, who had besieged the fort with forces of 30,000 horse and 300 elephant. In this battle the most famous of the Tomar chiefs, Man Singh, died; his son, Vikramaditya, held out for a year before acknowledging defeat. Fighting on the Sultan's losing side against Babur at Panipat in 1526, Vikramaditya was killed and Gwalior fell to the Moghuls, belonging to them (and briefly to Sher Shah) until 1754, when the Marathas took the fort.

In 1761, after the second battle of Panipat, the Jat Rana of Gohan, Bhim Singh, occupied Gwalior, only to lose it back to the Marathas in 1769. The British, in the person of Captain Popham, restored Gwalior to the Rana in 1780 but four years later Mahdaji Rao Scindia's armies, under de Boigne, recaptured the fort. Colonel White in 1804 reversed the procedure once more but the fort was ceded back to the Scindias the next year. (Both the British expeditions succeeded by taking the isolated south-west Ghargarjpaur or Ghargarj Gate, Popham by a daring climb with his men, and White by artillery bombardment from a mile away.)

The ancient hill fort of Gwalior.

OVERLEAF *Man Singh's Palace and Hathiyapaur, Elephant Gate.*

113

Man Singh's Palace showing ceramic
tilework, elephant screens and Hindu
corbelled arches on the outer walls.

In 1843 there was a mutiny but the British again restored Gwalior to the Scindias. Though Jayaji Rao and his minister, Sir Dinkar Rao, were not implicated, part of Jayaji Rao's forces joined the Great Mutiny of 1857–8. There was fierce fighting round Gwalior, between Tantia Topi and the recklessly courageous Rani of Jhansi, and the British. Eventually the fort was regained; Tantia Topi escaped for the time being but the Rani, wearing soldier's dress, was found among the dead. Gwalior was finally returned to the Scindias in 1885.

Gwalior is built on a high sandstone precipice 300 feet above the plain, and where the natural drop errs from the vertical the rock has been scarped to make it unscaleable. The steep, twisting ascent passes under the five palaces and, originally, it passed through seven gates; only five remain today. The imposing Hathiyapaur, the Elephant Gate, sixth in order, forms part of the palace of the greatest Tomar chief, Man Singh, the oldest and undoubtedly noblest example of Hindu secular building. It is also called the Chit Mandir, or Painted Palace: the walls, in particular the windowless south wall, are covered with a profusion of coloured tiles – bands of mosaic candelabra, Brahmani ducks, elephants and peacocks – enamelled blue, rose, green and gold, lending an unsurpassed charm and elegance to the whole façade. The east face is 300 feet long, with five massive round towers beneath open-domed cupolas and a battlement of beautiful open lattice-work. The two-storeyed palace is arranged round two lovely courts like *liwans*, with the *zenana* quarters above; these lead to roof terraces and pavilions looking out over the ramparts and inward over the courts, through *jali*-screened galleries between deep *chadyas*. The underground chambers recall the *serdabs* of Persian palaces, provided for summer retreat; but at Gwalior these rooms came to be used as dungeons for prisoners of State: Aurangzeb, for example, had his brother Murad Baksh and his nephew Sulaiman Shikah incarcerated and executed here.

Apart from its natural defences Gwalior had a further natural advantage in its unlimited supply of water: the two together earned the fort the reputation of being, like Kalinjar, one of the most impregnable bastions of the north. There are many tanks and *baoris* or wells here, of which the Suraj Kund on the west side is by far the largest. Quite close to this reservoir is the 9th-century *Tel-ka Mandir*, an extraordinary rectangular *shakti*-cult shrine: 80 feet high, it is the tallest building in the fort.

Between the Ganesh Gate and the fifth, Lakshman Gate, is the Chaturbhuja Temple dating from the time of the Pratiharas in 876, and hewn from the solid rock; it is dedicated to Vishnu. South of Man Singh's Palace are the two 11th-century Sasbahu Temples. Only the *mandapas* remain, but these are finely carved and ornamented with groups of female dancers and figures of Vishnu; the larger has a fine 12-sided hall.

Exquisitely carved brackets and (opposite) capitals in the inner court.

117

Plan of Gwalior:
a. Alamgir Gate
b. Hindola Gate
c. Ganesh Gate
d. Lakshman Gate
e. Elephant Gate
f. Man Singh Mahal (and inset A)
g. Vikramaditya Mahal
h. Jahangiri Mahal
i. Shah Jahan Mahal
j. Bala Qila
k. Suraj Kund
l. Sasbahu Temples
m. Tel-ka Mandir
n. Gharghari Gate
o. Jain sculptures
p. Urwahi Gate

The unique vaulted chamber on the eastern side of Man Singh's Palace court.

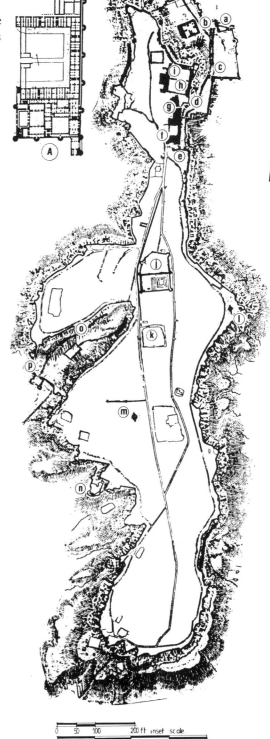

118

Sasbahu Temples.

Tel-ka Mandir.

On the eastern outskirt of the old city, which lies to the north and east of Gwalior's rock, is the tomb of a Muslim saint renowned as one of the finest early Moghul buildings in India. It is 100 feet square with hexagonal towers at the four corners attached at the angles to form an octagon. A high Pathan dome, once blue-glazed, surmounts a verandah with a central bay on each side, enclosed with *jali*-screens and protected by double *chadyas*. Nearby is the tomb of the musician, Tansen, one of the 'nine jewels' of Akbar's court.

Unquestionably one of Gwalior's most remarkable monuments are the five groups of colossal Jain rock sculptures, made in the cliff below the fortress walls. Most of these were mutilated by order of Babur in 1527, only 70 years after they were made; in his memoirs he records 'I directed these idols to be destroyed.' However, the broken heads have since been replaced with stucco. The principal figures among them are Adinath, the first Jain pontiff, known by the symbol of a bull or wheel; Nemnath, the 22nd pontiff, signified by a shell; and Siddhartha and Trisala, reputed parents of the infant Mahavira, last of the 24 pontiffs, whose symbol is a lion. They all date from the Tomar period, between 1440 and 1473.

Under the Raj, Gwalior saw some of the greatest tiger shoots in India; it is said of one Maharaja he was such a fine shot that his kills laid end to end would stretch for two and a half miles. Everything at Gwalior seems to be on a grand scale, but perhaps this is as it should be for a place that has borne such a large part in the making of India.

KALINJAR

Kalinjar – 'the most ancient fort in all Hindusthan'.

Kalinjar: lost in the mists of time, most ancient fort in all Hindusthan, unparalleled for its strength and invincibility. It stands on its famous hill, 800 feet up on the last spur of the Vindhya mountains, an awesome embodiment of Hindu power reaching back beyond recorded history to Vedic times. The crenellations of its grey serpentine walls seem to grow out of the very rock, belying in their grim visage the splendour and beauty of sculpture to be found within.

Many are the legends that surround the beginnings of this place. One ascribes the fort to Kalinjra, a son of King Bharata from whom India took its ancient name. Another proclaims Kalinjar as the abode of Lord Shiva. *Kal* means death and *jar* decay: thus the name exalts the god of destruction. But Kalinjar is inextricably linked to the fortunes of the Chandella kings of Jijhoti or Bundelkhand. The *Raisa*, the great epic poem of Chand Bardai, court poet to the Rajput Emperor Prithviraj Chauhan of Delhi, records how his master defeated the Chandellas in 1182, and tells the tale of their creation. The *Raisa* is to the Hindu spirit what Homer's *Iliad* was to the Greeks and is now to the Western mind. Even as Achilles was deemed the son of Apollo, born of Thetis, so Chandra Varman, the great Chandella warrior, was held to be the

Plan of Kalinjar:
a. Alamgir Gate
b. Ganesha Gate
c. Chandika Gate
d. Budh Bhadra Gate
e. Hakuman Gate
f. Red Gate (Lal Dawaza)
g. Swarg Rohan
h. Panna Gate
i. Kot Tirtha
j. Budha Bhadra
k. Neel Kantha and Kal Bhairav

121

Ribbed crenellations and natural ramparts top the huge hill on which Kalinjar stands at 800 feet.

mortal heir of Chandrama, the moon, and Hemavati, a Brahman maiden. At the entrance to Kalinjar's Neel Kanth Temple, a polished black stone tablet, perhaps 10th-century, declares the Chandella lineage.

The history of Kalinjar moves in half-light till the second half of the 10th century. The Chandel rajas were already independent and their King Dhanga joined a Hindu confederacy to repel an Afghan invasion led by Amir Sabuktigrin. His son, Mahmud Ghazni, the idol breaker, amassed vast plunder from his raids into India. He made at least 17 between 997 and 1027, starting out in October for three months' marching to the provinces of the Ganges and returning at the start of the hot season. In 1019 he crossed the Jumna and menaced Kalinjar. Its Chandel raja, Ganda, faced him with 36,000 horse, 45,000 foot and 640 war elephants. Neither side could claim a victory and in 1022 Mahmud returned, desirous of booty and the coveted title of Kalin-jaradhipati, Lord of Kalinjar, of more worth to conquerors than any treasure. Elephants, gold and jewels he received in gift from Ganda, and with those Mahmud retired from the field and from the history of Kalinjar.

Successive Muslim invasions weakened the fort's defences, and then

ABOVE AND BELOW LEFT *Hindu rock carvings on the tortuous ascent to the summit.*

Swarg Rohan, one of Kalinjar's seven gates.

in 1182 the rival Chandella forces were crushed by the Hindu Chauhan Emperor. In 1203 Kalinjar fell to the Muslim hosts of Qutb-ud-din Aibak, first of Delhi's slave dynasty, who defeated by siege the last of the Chandel rajas, Parmadideva. The sanctity of Kalinjar was violated. Zealous in their sack and destruction of the infidel fortress, the Muslims laid waste a rich and precious prize, blind to its glories, ignorant of its meaning.

The steep and stony route up to the fort is hard work even for peaceable visitors. Most castles and forts of the ancient world were allied to portents and manifestations of a greater power than man's. The way to Kalinjar is crossed by seven gates in varying styles, all of them guarded by barbicans of sorts, and seven in allusion to the seven known planets and the stations through which the soul must pass in aspiring to absorption in Brama: the second gate is called Swarg Rohan, the Heaven-ascending Gate.

Sculpted figures of Ganesha, Chandika and Hanuman, the Monkey God, lend their names to other gates. Black-faced monkeys swing lithely from the branches of trees roundabout: considered sacred to Hanuman, they live here unmolested. There are rock carvings to marvel at on the

Neel Kanth Temple; four heads crown each of the carved columns of the mandapa.

Two of the Kalinjar's most venerable ancient lingams: one in the temple's inner sanctum and another outside.

climb, worn images that once stood watch over resplendent palanquins, gilded elephants and royal cavalcades of archers and swordsmen bearing their glittering standards and proud emblems.

At the crest, turning from views of farming countryside, crumbling Hindu and Muslim monuments stand side by side on the mile-long plateau where once Chandella armies assembled: *chattris* and shrines with minarets, the palaces of queens, with *jali*-work or onion domes and lotus frieze. The Patal Ganga, or underground Ganges, runs through Kalinjar, through a cave carved with holy images. The waters of the Bhuriya Tal and Koth Tirth are said to have curative powers. Several *ghats* lead down to Koth Tirth and its tall, unexpected palm tree; the small mandir close by is still tended by a *pujari*. Sita Kund is named after Lord Rama's wife and Mrig Dhara, Deer Spring, wells up from the rocks, a fountain of clear, cool water.

Near the Koth Tirth mandir are the ruins of King Aman Singh's palace; its courtyard, bordered by two rows of peacock arches and once the scene of graceful dancing, is peopled differently now. Priceless stone relics are ranged everywhere, collected from all over the site: beautiful heads; languorous torsoes; a dancing Ganesha; Nandi bulls in profusion; a model temple complete with figures like a miniature Khajurao; a reclining Shiva – on and on this amazing display of rare and rarely seen sculpture lies like an embodiment of the legend: *kal, jar*.

From a gateway in the preserved inner curtain wall two flights of steps lead down to Kalinjar's holiest place, the Neel Kanth Temple of Shiva. There are weathered inscriptions and marvellous rock carvings to be seen on the way down: a toppled figure with the face of Hanuman, a boar incarnation of Vishnu, a superb lifesize dancing Ganesha wearing ankle bells, sinuous, pot-bellied and utterly captivating. Outside the sanctuary is an early hexagonal *mandapa* or pavilion, roofless now but with its exquisite pillars, capitals and mouldings still in place. Inside the cave is the blue stone *lingam* with silver eyes, object of veneration for more than 1000 years. A carved stone frieze tells stories from Hindu mythology, redolent of a fertile and all-encompassing culture. There is a sense that life holds its breath in this cave; it is very far from earthly things.

A giant Kal Bhairav is cut into the rock face nearby: Shiva in his opposite, destroyer, form, with 18 arms holding a sword, a skull, decorated with snake armlets, and a serpent twining round the neck. A carving of the goddess Kali stands close by; water seeping from a spring runs over both statues, imparting a lifelike glisten to the stony flesh.

Suttee pillars are scattered about the fort, mute reminders of self-immolation by Rajput women. No doubt they drew added courage from the example of Sati, wife to Shiva: shamed by an insult offered to her

husband by her father, she leapt into consuming flames in the presence of the assembled gods, was regenerated and reunited with Shiva as Parvati.

Kalinjar was retaken by the Hindus from the Slave Kings and remained theirs till 1545 when the Afghan Sher Shah besieged the fort. Each side took a savage battering, in the course of which Sher Shah was mortally wounded. He lived long enough to know of his troops' victory; the Hindu king, Kirat Singh, was executed. Humayun re-established Moghul rule in India and the forces of his son Akbar took Kalinjar in 1569. One of the daughters of Kirat Singh, Durgavati, was married to a raja of the Gonds, an ancient branch of the Chandel dynasty, and throughout her lifetime she battled against Akbar's armies to preserve her Hindu kingdom. She is as much the heroine of Bundelkhand as the Rani Lakshmi Bai of Jhansi.

Towards the end of Aurangzeb's reign the Bundela leader Chattrasal took Kalinjar. On his death in 1732 he bequeathed a third of his domains to the Marathas in recompense for past alliance, and Kalinjar remained part of the Panna State until surrendered to the British in 1812. The ancient Kalinjar hill, situated within reach of the holy river Ganges, has always been a place of pilgrimage and worship for *Rishis*, *Saddus* and holy men, but is rarely visited by other travellers. Few would manage the climb up to explore its wonders. The journey down is just as precarious, or more so, since darkness will fall before the village firelight and lamplight can be reached. Then Kalinjar will have melted into the black of night, insubstantial as legend, and as potent.

OPPOSITE *Kalinjar is endowed with long neglected masterpieces of Chandella sculpture: a dancing Ganesha forms a pillar in a doorway, and fragments of an enormous granite goddess, now toppled and abandoned.*

RIGHT *Kal Bhairav – Shiva in the form of the destroyer – a giant figure hewn from solid rock stands in one of the fort's perennial springs.*

AJAIGARH

Ajaigarh Fort with the town below.

Ajaigarh has rich rewards for the traveller unafraid of distance, difficulty and danger. Reached at last deep in rough and rugged country, the challenge is not yet ended: Ajaigarh's uneven rampart is an aching 800-foot climb from the plain and nearly three miles round, enclosing a triangular spur.

The views are breathtaking but Ajaigarh's treasures are to be found even before the topmost gate. On a huge cliff face are magnificent Hindu rock carvings – a cow and calf and innumerable *suttee* hands. Years of erosion by wind and water have damaged these exquisite sculptures but they remain an awe-inspiring revelation of a vanished civilisation. Strewn amongst the ruins lie a thousand broken and fragmented icons:

a dancing Ganesha so lyrical of line one can almost hear the ankle bells in graceful rhythm; a colossal Shantinath, one of the Jain pontiffs; the potent images of Durga and Kali; an ancient black stone statue of Vishnu.

Ajaigarh's thick battlemented walls never have the same depth or breadth for three yards running; Muslim handiwork is detectable in the haphazard implanting along the parapets of beautifully carved pillars and doorjambs from Hindu and Jain temples. With its great bastions and four large water caverns, Ajaigarh was a self-contained forest hill fort, meant to withstand long sieges and able to shelter the whole region's population within its walls. Huge blocks of stone once formed steps for elephants on the steep path to the main entrance, the Kalinjar Darwaza; a few of them remain, but of the five massive gateways only two are accessible now.

The Chandella kings of Jijhoti, or Bundelkhand, came to prominence in about 850 when they overthrew the Pratiharas; the fort takes its name from the sage, Ajaypala, who lived on its Kedar Parvat hill. Their main defensive bases were Kalinjar and Mahoba but by the 11th century Raja Kirtivarman had considerably extended their frontiers; the lake, Kirtisagar, was named after him. The 20th and last Chandella king was Parmidideva, reigning from 1167 to 1182 when he was defeated by the Chauhan Emperor of Delhi, Prithviraj, and lost Mahoba. Later, after the Chauhan's defeat by the Muslims, Qutb-ud-din conquered Kalinjar in 1203, and the Chandellas were confined to the region around Ajaigarh.

Today, Parmadi's lovely Parmal Tal is the most evocative place: tier upon tier of elaborately carved stones taper gently upwards and though doomed to slow decay, it conjures up a lost age of splendour and beauty. All around Ajaigarh's acres are *suttee* pillars, marked with the traditional symbols – sun, moon, a palm, a bangle; a *suttee* will be remembered for as long as there is a sun and a moon; her palm print carries blessing and her bangle is the sign of a married woman, for no *suttee* is ever considered a widow.

The craftsmen of Ajaigarh worshipped the rising sun as the mystic world, the lotus, carving its petals on pillars, arches and soaring *shikharas*. Panels and friezes of voluptuous nymphs and celestial *apasaras* recall the romantic and heroic sagas of the Chandella court bards about the many loves of Parmadi, about the valour of his two Banaphar Rajput warriors, Allha and Udal.

After the death of Parmadideva in 1213 the Chandellas declined still further. When Chattrasal, the Bundela chief, rose to power in Bundelkhand in the 18th century he took Kalinjar, and Ajaigarh. After his death in 1732 a period of confusion followed until the Nawab of Banda, Ali Bahadur, was victorious in his six-week struggle for the fort in 1800. Eight years later Lakshman Daowa captured Ajaigarh and

A rock-cut Ganesha now lies half-buried in the earth.

Carved in a huge cliff, figures worship Shiva lingams.

showed no signs of acknowledging the British presence in Bundelkhand. In 1809 the battle lines were drawn.

Under Colonel Martindell, the British Indian army took the surrounding hills in fierce fighting. Then they brought their artillery to bear: 'So heavy and destructive was the fire, that the enemy could not shew a man, and fired in the interval while our guns were cooling. By sunset two of their guns were dismounted and three of the gates, with their defences, laid in ruins. Immense masses of stone and masonry were brought down. Next morning, the batteries played on the upper gate and defences with powerful effect, and at noon the enemy displayed a white flag. At four they evacuated the fort; and at five we occupied it.'

Today the forest ranks of teak and ebony are moving in on Ajaigarh in a slower, silent battle to win the ruined walls and broken gods.

MAHOBA

& CHARKHARI

Charkhari hill fort.

OPPOSITE AND LEFT *The main entrance to the fort with its spiked Elephant Gate and gold sun and moon finials.*

The fort's Kali Temple and a marble multi-armed Kali murti *inside.*

The Chandella kings desired two earthly things after the safe possession of Bundelkhand: to build temples for their gods and to bring water to their land. These two desires find perfect union at Mahoba, the Bundela capital, for there, on an island in Madan Sagar, stands one Shiva temple called Vijai Varman that has remained unspoilt since the 12th century.

All the other temples – and palaces – at Mahoba have been in ruins since the Muslim invasions, not just as a result of battle but because 'the destruction of a Hindu temple furnished the destroyer with the ready means of building a house for himself on earth, as well as in heaven . . . in none of the cities which the early Muhammadans occupied permanently, have they left a single temple standing, save this solitary

135

The lake or tal, viewed from the ramparts, skirts the fort on three sides.

temple at Mahoba, which doubtless owed its preservation solely to its secure position and the deep waters of the Madan Sagar.' The island may only be reached today by courtesy of the local people, who will paddle a visitor across the lake in a dug-out canoe.

There are discoveries to be made all around this countryside: a dancing Ganesha of whitewashed granite propped against a tree in a mustard field; a sun temple dedicated to Surya; the vast figure of

An abandoned cannon still on its original carriage.

The island temple in the Madan Sagar at Mahoba.

An ancient rock-cut Kal Bhairav
murti polished black with oil.

Shiva cut into some rocks and gaily painted; a temple shrine housing a
Kal Bhairav *murti* cut from polished black stone. Ancient *ghats* – steps
leading to a waterside bathing place – stand alongside temples round
a huge tank; curiously, amid so much ruin one can more easily imagine
the people of the past who lived their lives in these surroundings.

The Chandellas made four lakes by damming valleys. Madan Sagar,
about three miles round, was made in the 12th century and deep Vijay
Sagar in the 11th: this is the longest lake, about 4 miles round; the
other two are Kalyan Sagar and Kirat Sagar. These lakes were certainly
not created for their picturesque effect, nor only for the irrigation
works they made possible and which are still in use today: defence was
always a consideration, and the Chandellas' *giri durg* or hill fort at
Charkhari is surrounded on three sides by water.

The landward approach to the fort is made through an imposing gate,
its door studded with lethal spikes. Beautiful as well as functional, the
gate has three domes with gold sun and moon finials above *jali*-work
screen windows. It leads to a palace courtyard and a *durbar* hall
peopled with battered portraits of the Charkhari Rajas.

The onward path is a long, gradual climb to the fort's inner curtain
wall; long and gradual by design, so that elephants and heavy guns
could be brought up. Charkhari is a gunner's fort. There are cannons
abandoned in the dust of every bastion, cannons pointing from embrasures, and one colossus still housed, on its original carriage, in a
small, domed magazine. Within these stout defences are the temple
gardens, now gloriously overgrown, a *baori* or step well, and the temple
to one side of it, sheltering two marvellous 17th-century multi-armed
marble images of the warlike goddess, Kali.

Parmadidev, the last Chandella king, was defeated here by the
Chauhan Emperor, Prithviraj, in 1182. Qutb-ud-din came next and
after a long period of Muslim rule a new Bundela chief, Chattrasal, rose
up in the 18th century; his grandson, Khuman Singh, founded Charkhari state in 1765, and in 1804 Bijai Bahadur was one of the first Bundela
rulers to accept British overlordship. Charkhari was lost to the forces
of Tantia Topi during the Mutiny: 'Elephants and horses with their
trappings, carriages of various kinds, palanquins and other convey-
ances, camels and draught bullocks, the cattle belonging to the inhabitants, here all fell into the hands of the enemy.' After the Mutiny,
Raja Ratan Singh was awarded a hereditary salute of 11 guns, and a
perpetual *jaghir* or stipend.

The view from Charkhari's ramparts is spectacular, across the lakes
to marvellous wild-fowling country. A deserted Edwardian summer
palace, its whitewash streaking down grey walls, still holds echoes of
the great shooting parties that set out from here in horse-drawn *tongas*
and bullock carts, scattering flocks of goats down the tree-lined roads.

GARHKUNDAR

ising out of black granite rock in wild dacoiti country stands the foreboding fortress of Garhkundar. A remarkably austere stronghold, standing foursquare on its hill, it commands a 360° view over the plains. Rarely visited by *ferenghi*, outsiders, since the days of the Raj and the occasional tour of a District Magistrate, Garhkundar has a romance and an allure all its own. It is the lair of wolves and wild boar and brigands, and the prudent visitor will venture forth in strength.

In the haze of distance the fort is softer-seeming, less foreboding.

BELOW AND OPPOSITE *Garhkundar Fort stands foursquare on its granite hill base.*

Silhouetted turrets and towers are visible for a while, yet with a turn or dip in the road they can hide completely and uncannily to confuse an enemy. Villages and cultivated fields hug the approach and then, quite sharply, the terrain becomes a scorched garden of black rocks and dead silver trees at the very foot of Garhkundar.

Conjecture places the origins of the Kundar stronghold in the 9th century. In the wake of Chandella kings, the Chauhan Emperor and the Delhi Sultans, numerous short-lived dynasties fought savagely for land and probably in the late 12th century Khub Singh of the Khangar clan seized large tracts of Jijhoti, or Bundelkhand, and established a capital at Garhkundar. The Khangars were necessarily a bold and ferocious people, constantly engaging in campaigns and raids for land and plunder. Khub Singh accumulated great treasure and with it built ever-widening rings of citadels as his domains increased, dextrously playing off the ambitions of his *jaghirdars*, liegemen, against each other.

Unfettered passions brought the downfall of the Khangars and of Garhkundar. Hurmat Singh Khangar's ambition was to marry his son Nagdeva to the daughter of Sohanpal, one of the Rajput Bundelas. The Rajput clans split cleanly in two: some would help Sohanpal resist the upstart Khangar overlord from Hamirpur and some would not. Constraints of hospitality were unknown: Sohanpal and his adherents murdered Hurmat Singh and Nagdeva while they were sleeping off the wedding feast. Though Sohanpal annexed Hamirpur and became the most powerful Bundela leader, the split between the clans remained and proved a fatal weakness in opposing the imperial Tughluq forces of the 14th century.

Many times the Delhi Sultans had tried to remove the thorn of an independent Hindu kingdom, but Garhkundar's isolation and inhospitable terrain had defeated them. Now, with dissension in the Bundela confederacy, the Tughluqs forced the issue and again a woman was the unlucky, ostensible cause of conflict.

Bardai Singh Khangar of Garhkundar had a beautiful daughter, Kesar Devi: knowing what would be the answer, the Muslim Sultan asked for her in marriage. The siege of Garhkundar dragged out long and grim and ended in *johar*. When the Tughluq armies retired, the entire Khangar dynasty was dead, their temples and shrines sacked and plundered, their city and their fort in ruins.

The story of Garhkundar ended then, but the bleak fields of Bundelkhand hid a secret from the world for many centuries. Among the rough and overgrown stones and boulders and fallen masonry were found the venerable *suttee* pillars of sun and moon and bangled hand: only then was it known that Garhkundar had indeed fallen to the Muslim Tughluqs and not to the neighbouring Bundela Rajputs, as had always been believed.

OPPOSITE *Entrance front and courtyard of the Bundela Palace within the fort.*

The pillars were found at the foot of the citadel; at its entrance lies a long cannon, immovable in the dust, then the way leads through an arched chamber into a large square courtyard with square corner towers. The three storeys are easily explored; the dungeons are another matter – immense and dark and bat-ridden, they would terrify all but the most intrepid treasure-seeker. Garhkundar's one treasure now is the staggering array of views from the parapets. The immensity of India is here graphically displayed – lakes, green and brown fields like a giant's chequerboard, jungle villages, a distant *chattri* dancing like a mirage on the horizon. The windows of Garhkundar gaze emptily, where once its possessors were lords of all they surveyed.

Parvati, flanked by her sons Ganesha and Kartikeya, guards the rugged road to Garhkundar.

A suttee *pillar showing sun, moon and hand for immortality.*

ORCHHA

Jehangiri Mahal, Ramji Mandir and Raj Mahal on Orchha's island in the Betwa river.

The bold silhouettes of Orchha symbolise for all time the power and panache of the Bundela Rajas: every curve and contour flaunts the pomp and circumstance of this adventurous breed. Garhkundar, once the capital of Bundelkhand, had fallen to the Tughluqs just as that dynasty was weakening. Into the vacuum they left expanded the Bundela clans, moving their base early in the 16th century from the wilderness to the banks of the Betwa. Raja Rudra Pratap threw a wall round the existing settlement here, once an outpost of Malwa's Chanderi, and built a bridge to the island citadel, the Ramji Mandir, as it came to be called, first of Orchha's three great palaces. Before his death — he died rescuing a cow from a tiger — Rudra Pratap also began work on the Raj Mahal, continued by his successor, Bharti Chand, and completed by the great Madhukar Shah.

The true fortunes of the House of Orchha may be said to stem from the talent, practised by certain of its enterprising scions, of gaining the goodwill of their imperial counterparts. Though he was defeated in battle by Akbar, the third Moghul Emperor, the indomitable Madhukar Shah presented himself at the imperial court wearing a huge vermilion *tilak* on his forehead, a marking expressly forbidden by Akbar. Friendship, not punishment, sprang from this proud entry, and the same kind of pride marks the buildings of Madhukar Shah at Orchha.

Madhukar Shah belonged to the Krishna *bhakti* cult of Hinduism, a new concept of congregational worship that may have come about in reaction to the crusading fervour of Islam. Certainly the Bundela temples at Orchha are a miraculous embodiment of light and space, utterly different from the dark and narrow confines of traditional temple interiors intended only for the priests and for the chosen elect of worshippers. The Chatturburj Temple built between 1558 and 1573 is as vast as any European cathedral, an enormous cruciform hall with a domed crossing and soaring *shikaras* at the four corners and over the sanctuary.

Dwarfed by this creation is the famous Ram Raja Temple. Legend has it that this was never intended as a temple but had been completed as a palace by Madhukar Shah for his wife, Rani Ganesh. She had journeyed to the holy river Saryu at Ayodhaya, her dynastic seat, to pray to Rama. After a year's devotions the god consented to return with her to Orchha, provided she made the journey there on foot with his image and installed it in a palace like a raja, never to be moved. Many months later, on her return to Orchha, the Rani placed Rama's icon in her palace till its temple should be ready, but even after the completion of the great Chatturburj, it refused to budge. An image of Lord Vishnu had to be placed within the temple meant for his *avatar* Rama, and the Rani's palace became the dynastic temple, the Ramji Mandir. Thousands of pilgrims journey here every year.

It is very probable that the wall and ceiling paintings of the Raj Mahal were begun during the reign of Madhukar Shah. They all portray religious mythology, a profusion of *avatars*, saints and *apasaras* telling the stories of the *Ramayana*, vivid drama in strong colour. This period was one of important artistic development, of great works not only in architecture and painting but in poetry too. At Madhukar Shah's court, and at two of his successors', lived the Brahman poet Keshodas, whose *Ram Chandrika* is considered one of the finest compositions in Hindu verse. His masterpiece on the art of poetry, *Kavi Priya*, was dedicated to a famous courtesan of Orchha, Praveen Rai, also a considerable poet whose songs and verses are still sung in Bundelkhand.

In 1598 Madhukar Shah died, to be succeeded by his ineffectual brother, Ram Singh. However, imperial events again took a hand in the affairs of Orchha. One of Akbar's sons, Prince Murad, died of drink in 1599, leaving Daniyal and the eldest son, Salim, as contenders for their father's empire. In 1601 Salim, the child of so many prayers at Fatehpur Sikri, rebelled against his father and the following year instigated the

Exterior and interior court of the Jehangiri Mahal.

murder of one of the 'nine jewels' of Akbar, his father's greatest friend and minister, Abu-l Fazl, whom the prince hated and feared. The man he chose for the deed was Bir Singh Deo of Orchha, younger brother to the ruler, Ram Singh.

In 1604 Prince Daniyal died, of drink like his brother Murad. Salim, intimidated by his father and the threat that one of his own sons, Khusru, would be made heir apparent, stayed at court in Agra, biding his time. Akbar died in 1605 and Salim succeeded as the Emperor Jehangir. One of his first acts was to remove Ram Singh to Chanderi and recall Bir Singh from his fugitive existence to rule over Orchha.

The energy of Bir Singh was prodigious and found new expression in his settled life: he was the moving force behind some outstanding architectural and artistic landmarks in a synthesis of Hindu and Muslim styles, not just here at Orchha but at Datia, at Jhansi and innumerable other forts all over Bundelkhand. Had he only built at Orchha he would be remembered.

The Lakshmi Narayan Temple, combining the architecture of temple and fort, is marvellously painted with stories of Hindu mythology, full

147

Rich tilework on the Ramji Mandir. *Raj Mahal and the river front.*

Jehangiri Mahal: a corner pavilion with galleries and chattris.

of sensitive colourwork and fine detail. But Bir Singh's epitaph is the magnificent Jehangiri Mahal, named for his benefactor. This imposing palace is built in five receding storeys surmounted by the domed and balconied kiosks of the roof terraces, like the ancient Hindu *prasada*. The sandstone façade is covered in painted peacocks, floral designs and geometric patterns, the once vibrant colours much faded. Screen windows with delicate *jali*-work overlook the Betwa; eaves and piers are carved with flowers like a lace covering. The main entrance is flanked by sculpted elephants, and elephant brackets within uphold the russet cornice of the great courtyard. Once, light was reflected from the central fountain onto the creamy *kauri* or crushed shell plastered walls of the pavilions, decorated with carved blossoms spun into tendrils and arabesques. The finely worked arcades, the splendid domes, have that air of grace and harmony depicted in the enchanting paintings of the *Ras Lila* of Lord Krishna: *gopis* and dancing girls, lovebirds darting in the pearly shadows.

The garden here was made on Moghul lines, its cool canals making four smaller square gardens that would have added their scent and colour to the beauty of the pavilions. The Phool Bagh, Flower Garden, Palace is nearby, built for Bir Singh's sons: an airy *baradari* or audience hall linked by a wide terrace to the *zenana*. There were as many rooms below the hall as above it, kept deliciously cool in summer by labyrinthine water pipes fed from two water towers or *sawan bhadar*. Orchha is famously haunted and walking in these gardens, amid the stir and rustle of leaves, with shadows playing along the walls, imagination calls the spirits forth.

Bir Singh died in 1627 and the vainglorious Jhujan Singh took his place. He was remarkable only as the unwitting cause of his younger brother's immortal memory. Suspecting his Rani of infidelity, Jhujan ordered her to bring poisoned food to Dewan Hardaul. She, chaste but proud, declined to countenance such an admission of guilt but Hardaul,

Ceiling paintings of the developed phase of the Bundelkhand school showing everyday life in a fort.

149

The pepper pots and domes of the Orchha fort complex seen from the Chatturburj Temple. Edwin Lutyens was inspired by these in his building of New Delhi.

determined to scotch his brother's slander and spare the Rani shame, willingly partook of the poisoned meal, and died. Even today, in the villages of Bundelkhand, many houses have a shrine for Hardaul and here at Orchha his cenotaph or *samadhi* marks the place of his sacrifice.

In 1628 Jhujan rebelled against Shahjahan but was forced to submit and to pay heavily in money and land for his foolhardiness. For several years he served in the Deccan but the grant of title to Raja whetted his ambition and, ignoring Shahjahan's orders, in 1634 he defeated and treacherously slew the neighbouring chief of Chauragarh. The imperial

150

Memorial chattris *of the Orchha kings on the banks of the Betwa river.*

army routed Jhujan; fleeing, he was killed in the jungle by Gonds, and Orchha was pillaged.

Bir Singh's other son, Baghwan Rao, had followed in the tradition of his line with courage and bravura, and in 1626 had founded a new kingdom at Datia. In 1783 the Bundela capital was moved to Tikamgarh, leaving Orchha to the jade green *dhak* forests, the sun-dappled waters of the Betwa and its auspicious guardian eagles. This marvellous creation is now terribly neglected, barely known and hardly seen by anyone when it should surely rank as one of the jewels of India.

151

DATIA

Datia Fort and section and plan of the four-storeyed Govind Mahal.

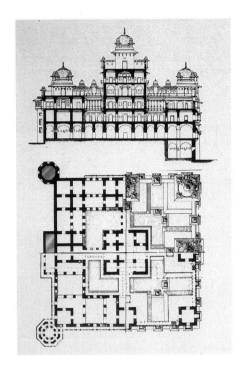

Lutyens described the fortress palace at Datia as 'one of the most interesting buildings architecturally in the whole of India'. It is an exemplary alliance of the Rajput and Moghul building arts, and bears the clear stamp of one man upon it, the Bundela chief, Bir Singh Deo.

The early part of his story is told in the history of Orchha, how he supported Crown Prince Salim's antagonism towards his father, the Emperor Akbar, by killing Akbar's friend and Salim's supposed detractor, Abu-l Fazl. This he did in 1602 at Antri near Gwalior, while Abu-l Fazl was returning from a successful campaign in the Deccan with a camel train of treasure. Though he was a fugitive from Akbar's wrath until the Emperor's death in 1605, it was widely supposed that Bir Singh found some means to hide the treasure and later used it to finance his building schemes at Orchha and at Datia.

Unlike most Moghul palaces, Datia was conceived as a single unit: in form and design, in colour and ornamentation, the various parts of the building are completely integrated into an ebullient yet uniquely elegant creation. Built in 1620 on a rocky elevation, the five-storeyed palace appears much taller than its actual 130 feet. Its balconies, bridges and oriel windows provide attractive panoramas from any viewpoint, gracefully bound together by the symmetry of domes and kiosks, arcades and eaves on every side. It is a place to wander in, letting a sense of India take hold. Datia is haunted by the spirits of the past, that is sure; even in the midday heat an unaccountably chilling breeze passes through the courts.

153

The Govind Mahal central pavilion containing the raja's apartments.

Bir Singh never wavered in his loyalty to Jehangir. In 1625, when the Emperor was travelling to Kabul, he was seized by Mahabat Khan. Bir Singh sent one of his younger sons, Baghwan Rao, to Jehangir's aid and on his successful return made over to him a *jaghir* which included the town and palace of Datia. In 1626 Baghwan Rao took up residence as first king of the new, state, but spent comparatively little time in his capital. He was a fighter and constantly on the move: subduing the rebellious Khan Jehan Lodi, aiding Asat Khan in the Bijapur campaign, quelling the governor's uprising at Lahore. He died in 1656; his *samadhi*, the Surahi Chattri, stands near the town.

Subha Karan succeeded his father. He fought 22 battles as far afield as Badakshan and Arazan, and showed all his forbears' flair for judging the outcome of a dispute when he placed his forces behind Aurangzeb in the succession battles between Shahjahan's four sons. He was made Subahdar of Bundelkhand on Aurangzeb's accession in 1659. Fighting for Aurangzeb involved several campaigns against the Marathas, during one of which, in 1679, Subha Karan died of an illness. Dalpat Rao had already distinguished himself with his father against the Marathas and was received with great honour by Aurangzeb at court,

154

A corner pavilion and one of the side pavilions linked with the central pavilion by elegant bridges and colonnades at upper and lower levels.

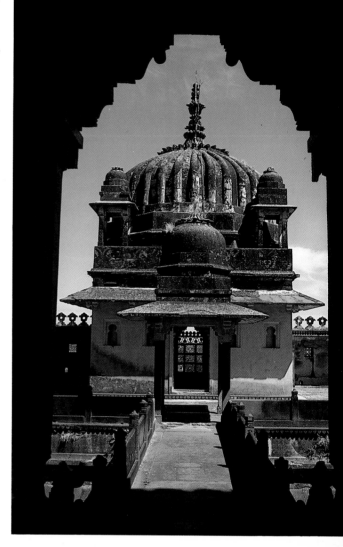

becoming one of his trusted lieutenants. After his valorous part in the siege of Gingee in 1694, the Emperor presented him with two massive gates which were installed in the Phool Bagh at Datia. Dalpat Rao died in the battle of Jajau in 1707, the year of Aurangzeb's death.

Adherence to the Moghuls had automatically brought the Bundelas into sharp conflict with the Marathas. During the last years of Aurangzeb, Moghul administration was weak and Bundelkhand became a free-for-all ground where local chiefs and Rajas grabbed what they could and fought to hold it. Datia, under Shatrujit, sided against the Maratha Scindias of Gwalior; only the superior strategy of the Scindias' French general, Perron, won the day for the Marathas, and Shatrujit was killed. Parichat, his son, succeeded him in 1801 and in 1804, rather than go over to the Marathas, he made a treaty of alliance with the British and ushered in an era of comparative peace. Parichat is credited with having built the city wall, with its four massive gates that take their name from the towns towards which they face: Richhara, Lashkar, Bhander, and Jhansi.

In 1818 Datia played host to the British Governor-General, Lord Hastings, and a splendid *durbar* was held in 1902 for the Viceroy, Lord Curzon. But by then the princes had long found it impossible to maintain such state, and Datia had already lain deserted for more than 60 years.

SAMTHAR

Samthar Fort seen from the air.

The three-tiered walls from across the moat.

The great moated *nara durg* of Samthar has barely seen a shot fired in anger. Broadly contemporary with the fighting Sikh fort at Patiala, its magnificent three-tiered battlements and powerful gun emplacements are a statement of intention never put to the test: the fort's huge iron elephant gates stand open now as they did in the time of Samthar's most dramatic hour, when the Maharani ordered sanctuary for British residents fleeing death during the Mutiny of 1857–8.

Samthar was India's only Gujar state. The Gujars, great warriors, had come with the hordes of Huns in the 5th century to settle in Gujarat and elsewhere in Rajputana. The Samthar ruler belonged to the Bar-Gujar clan, a sect which was included in Colonel Tod's 19th-century study as one of India's 36 royal races. Claiming descent from an illustrious line already old when Alexander entered India, Chandrabhan Bar-Gujar had become a governor in Baghwan Rao's new state of Datia in the 17th century, gradually increasing his possessions and influence. By the end of the 18th century his great-grandson, Madan Singh, had allied himself to the Marathas when they invaded Datia, and with their help formed the breakaway state of Samthar. In 1817, after the Marathas' defeat, Raja Madan Singh signed a treaty with the British.

Once assured of British protection, the Rajas bent their energies to vying with one another for precedence at court, but peaceably. The restrained official report of the Agra *durbar* of 1866 noted: 'The gratification afforded to the Treaty Chiefs of Bundelkhand, Datia, Orchha and Samthar was somewhat marred by a feeling of mortification at the position assigned them with reference to some of the Princes of Rajputana of modern creation . . . no definite decision has yet been given as to the exact position they are to occupy at future similar *durbars*, the conflicting claims and pretensions of the several chiefs doubtless making the settlement of this point a delicate and difficult matter.' It was perhaps fortunate that any title elevation for loyalty to the Queen-Empress was dependant upon practical matters, like the introduction of forward-looking programmes for famine and drought relief.

However, building has always formed a part of such plans and at Samthar the years of Pax Britannica after the Mutiny saw the addition of administrative blocks and courts for European visitors. An Italian, known locally as 'Tonton Sahib', is credited with building the seven-

Jaghirdars *in the Maharaja's forecourt await an audience.*

159

storeyed fort palace, easily the tallest building for several hundred square miles and dwarfing the old amalgam of temples, courts of audience, *zenanas*, gardens and elephant houses.

Royal patronage in the form of construction was essential for temples, schools and hospitals as well as the more traditional support of artists, poets and musicians. The Rajas still maintained their courts, celebrating the Id and Holi festivals with their peoples; there were elephant processions with spearmen and lancers and fireworks; the gardens were well looked after; a menagerie was maintained; there were *shikar*, tennis, cricket and horse-riding and, though *purdah* was still enforced, there was a specially curtained track built so that the ladies could bicycle.

Today, the menagerie still houses a panther and some deer, though there is a government farm here, too. The fort is still lived in by the Samthar family, along with more than 200 *karindars*, feudal retainers, who live here rent free, keeping up their ties with the old days. There is still a resident *pundit*, who divines the royal horoscopes and decrees auspicious periods. Water is still provided by *panharis* with leather bottles strapped to their backs. Candles still light the way at dusk. Dancing girls are still invited from the villages. India is still India.

160

ABOVE *Italianate seven-storeyed palace apartments.*

RIGHT *Raj Mandir which houses the family deities.*

LEFT *Aerial view of the principal entrance.*

JHANSI

The visitor to Jhansi comes not so much to view the walls and battlements and deserted terraces as to be touched by the spirit of place. Jhansi Fort has become the *chattri* of the woman who headed the Indian troops here during the Mutiny of 1857–8, the Rani Lakshmi Bai.

The nucleus of the present fort was built in 1613 by Bir Singh Deo of Orchha, though local lore telling of an earlier site here is borne out by carved stonework, set within the walls, of the 12th- and 13th-century Chandella period. These walls, with their ten gates, towers, bastions and battlements, march across the brown hillsides to surround the old city.

The policy of the British in India affected Jhansi in two main ways. The first was part of the question of paramountcy and independent

possession of land and honours before the British arrival; the second was the question of 'the doctrine of lapse', that is, an annexation policy where there was no direct heir, the British having the power to decide as necessary whether or not to accept the princely Hindu practice of adoption. In many cases, where rulers were confirmed in their positions, they had no incentive to further their state, neither could they take part in government. In other cases, where states were annexed under the doctrine of lapse, even the titles were abolished.

In 1853 Raja Gangadhar Rao of Jhansi died without a direct heir. His adopted son was not recognized and his widow, the Rani Lakshmi Bai, reluctantly at first and then with fiery courage took on the British in the unsettled years leading up to the Mutiny.

The Mutiny began with a massacre at Delhi in May 1857. Parts of Rajputana and Gwalior rose, as did Lucknow, Cawnpore, Benares – and Jhansi, where European officers and their families were massacred after surrender on the promise of protection, a repetition of what had happened at Cawnpore. After the second relief of Lucknow, the forces of Tantia Topi from Gwalior were scattered.

At Jhansi the Rani waited, hoping to be reinforced by Tantia Topi's army as she endured the siege of General Sir Hugh Rose. The Rani had come to Jhansi as Manu, spirited daughter of a poor Brahman of Varanasi. She was an inspired leader and united all castes and communities under her banner. Two of her most trusted gunners, Ghulam Gaus Khan and Khuda Baksh, were Muslim; they died defending the fort and are buried here. The great cannon they used are still on the ramparts – Radak-Bijli, Lightning, its nozzle carved like a lion's mouth, and Bhawani Shankar. Other brave and loyal women withstood the siege beside Lakshmi Bai – Jalkhari Dulaiya and Moti Bai, who died in the fight; she too is buried here.

Pacing the ramparts, now overgrown with bougainvillaea, praying in the mandir, patrolling her artillery, ordering a stockade to be built across a breach in the walls, Lakshmi Bai held Jhansi together. Three days after the breach, the fort fell. There was bitter hand-to-hand and door-to-door fighting between her forces and the British Indian army. Five thousand people died.

In the mêlée, the Rani and her adopted son escaped on horseback to join up with Tantia Topi and give battle again: 'We were sent all over the country in pursuit, and one of our troops overtook her at a place called Banda, 20 miles off. Her escort made a hard fight of it and though our fellows did their utmost and killed every man, she got away, her smart saddle falling into our hands. She is a wonderful woman, very brave and determined. It is fortunate for us that the men are not all like her.'

In a fierce fight on the 18th June 1858, at Kotah-ki-Sarai near Gwalior,

163

A Hindu shrine in the Rani's garden.

Concentric walls of the main entrance barbican.

The lion mouth of the Radak-Bijli, 'Lightning' cannon.

Lakshmi Bai, dressed like a man 'using her sword with both hands and holding the reins of her horse in her mouth' was killed. After the Mutiny Jhansi was occupied by the British, handed over in 1861 to Scindia of Gwalior, but returned again to the British in 1886.

The grave of many an Englishman lies in the dusty ground outside the city where General Sir Hugh Rose had his camp, all as young and as passionate as Lakshmi Bai. The whitewashed mandir at Jhansi Fort is still tended by a *pujari*, and of a dusky winter evening, as the dead leaves rustle down the steps, perhaps the visitor may catch a glimpse of 'the fleeting image of a shade'.

TALBEHAT

Talbehat presents two intriguingly different faces to the world: on the hill above the *bihat* or village, are the uncompromising, mile-long walls of unwelcome that withstood fierce sieges by Rajputs and Chandellas; above the *tal*, the fortress shows an altogether more open aspect, reflected in the waters of the lake that was the reason for the earliest settlement here.

Aboriginal Gonds ruled this hard, hot, hilly land after the breakup of Harsha Vardana's empire in the 7th century; their irrigation works are still fed by the *tal*. The 8th century saw first the Pratihara Rajputs and then the Chandellas take control – the main fortifications with earthworks and counterscarps probably date from that time – but the Gonds re-took Talbehat in the 12th century. From then until the 1800s Talbehat changed hands peacefully, most notably early in the reign of the Emperor Jehangir. At that time, 1605, Talbehat belonged to Orchha but wishing to reward his friend, Jehangir dispossessed the ruler Ram Singh in favour of Bir Singh Deo, compensating Ram Singh with the holding of Chanderi, and Talbehat formed part of the settlement.

Ram Singh's son, Bharat Sah, built much of the fort in 1618. The brickwork is thickly plastered, the inside walls with polished *kauri*, crushed shell, plaster in which peacock arches and lotus friezes can still be picked out. At the very top of the fort is the place where the women would sit, overlooking the lake, to enjoy the cooler air. Frescoes and rough carvings tell of ancient customs and record some of Talbehat's history. One group tells the story of a party of young girls, celebrating the Bundela Akti festival. Venturing too near the fortress walls, they were abducted and ravished by the garrison: rather than endure life dishonoured, the girls jumped to their deaths from the parapets.

One of the temples here is dedicated to Hanuman, the Monkey God, with a large bright orange image of him at the entrance. The temple with its vaulted roof is cut directly from the rock, its gods still standing in an inner sanctum and still tended by an old *pujari*: as in every Indian fort, no matter how battered, tumbledown or unkempt, one votive temple remains in use, an indestructible link between past and present.

Life in the fort, in peace or in siege, was sustained by water drawn from the deep, square, central *baori* with steps leading down to it from all sides. Three parallel flights of steps, all at different levels, descend to a triple-arched water gate by the *tal*, an unexplained and unexpected refinement, like a Gothick folly.

Situated so close to Jhansi, it was inevitable that Talbehat should become a rallying point in the battles of the Mutiny in 1857 and 1858. This whole region, guarded by so many lesser known fortresses, saw some of the grimmest fighting of those years. Eventually the British Indian army, under Sir Hugh Rose, stormed the fort – the breach at the outer gate can still be seen – and Talbehat was plundered and burnt.

166

The fort reflected in the lake or tal
from which it takes its name.

*The village sheltering in the
lea of the fort.*

The ramparts and water gate.

Three flights of steps at three different levels lead down from the fort to the lake, passing through a triple arch.

DEOGARH & CHANDER

The Kanalidurga of Deogarh. Jain images of the Mahavira and Tirthankaras cover the walls of the compound surrounding the Shantinath Temple complex.

Deogarh – Fort of the Gods – and Chanderi stand either side of the Betwa river on the main route to the Deccan. For nine centuries, armies with caravans in their wake have moved through this region, power shifting back and forth between Hindu and Muslim, each breaking and building anew.

Nothing can quite prepare the visitor for Deogarh. Perhaps the scale of its importance can best be conveyed by describing it as India's Ankor Watt. Within its ancient, broken curtain walls lie the remains of over 30 Jain temples, dating back mostly to the 9th and 10th centuries but in one case, a Varaha temple dedicated to the boar incarnation of Vishnu, probably dating as far back as the 5th century.

The fort is entered through a corbelled Hindu gateway in the outer walls. A path has been cleared through thick undergrowth and a kind of rubble – except that here the stones and masonry everywhere to be seen are the broken and defaced statuary and images sacred to this place, destroyed in repeated Muslim occupations.

The *murti*, images of gods and goddesses, line or sometimes are stuck into both the outside and inside of the walls that border the main temple. Some figures are standing; others are dancing or in the lotus position. Each one is varied in its jewellery or its way of dressing the hair, but all are characterised by the astonishing skill in carving inherited from the Gupta period, reckoned 'in the annals of classical India almost what the Periclean age is in the history of Greece'. Beauty, grace, restraint, refinement adorn Deogarh, hewn out in granite or the softer red and grey sandstone.

The main temple area is now enclosed and protected, with a venerable custodian of the keys. Just below the fort in a field by a well, not far from the banks of the Betwa, is the jewel of Deogarh, the Vishnu Dashavatara Temple, certainly 6th-century but very probably early 5th, bearing as it does an inscription attributable to Govinda, Viceroy of Malwa for his brother, the great Emperor Kumaragupta I.

This temple is probably the earliest surviving example of a Hindu sanctuary chamber with the *shikhara*, receding stone superstructure, representing the *prasada* or mansion of the gods. One face contains the carved doorway, the other three some of the world's greatest sculpture, including the famed Vishnu Narayana. There are four free-standing pillars entirely carved with Sahastra Kuta in the lotus position; next, a domed hexagonal building on pillars with capitals carved as gods accompanying their singing on musical instruments. A pillared hall precedes the sanctuary – the *garghgriha* or womb – which holds the main idol, here a gigantic black-painted statue of Shantinath, one of the Jain pontiffs whose symbol, as at Gwalior, is an antelope. Worshippers still make the pilgrimage to venerate the gods of Deogarh, as they have done for 1500 years.

171

The court of the Shantinath Temple complex within the fort contains pillars carved with Sahastra Kuta in the lotus position.

A corbelled Hindu gateway in the curtain wall of the fort.

172

The famous Vishnu Narayana sculpture on the Dashavatara Temple.

A fallen idol and Jain images set into the temple compound wall.

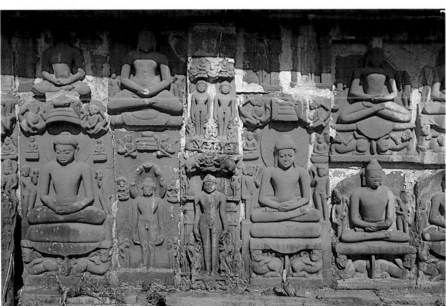

Chanderi: Babur's gorge in the Kirtidurga spur and Jain images cut into the adjacent rock face.

OPPOSITE *Chanderi Fort: the Kirtidurga Palace complex and palatine mosque; interior.*

174

A place in heaven was assured for the slayer of infidels: *Ghazi* — Avenger of God. Babur, first of the Moghul Emperors, took this title when he took Chanderi in 1528. Descendant of Genghis Khan and Timur, Babur at the age of eleven had inherited a principality but had three times won and lost the kingdom of Samarkand before breaking through from Kabul into India. He was an outstanding general and he had, moreover, artillery, not previously known in northern India till the Battle of Panipat in 1526 and his defeat of Rana Sanga in 1527.

Medina Rao, lieutenant to the great Rana Sanga of Chitorgarh, clung to the idea of Rajput independence and spurned Babur's offer of a negotiated settlement. The siege of Chanderi lasted less than a month. The outer walls of the fort are granite formations: the breach made by Babur's guns is clearly visible, and through it the defending Rajputs streamed towards their death, leaving behind the grim *johar* of their children and womenfolk. Babur's army sacked Chanderi and slew the inhabitants; *chor minars*, grisly totems of victory, were posted round the countryside, pillars of plaster with 30 or 40 heads of infidels stuck into each.

Chanderi had been well established as a strategic holding by the 10th century, when it was controlled by the Pratihara kings; the artificial lake to the east, the Kirtisagar, is attributed to Kirtipala and the fort itself, with its four miles of walls, is still called Kirtidurga.

Early in the 13th century Chanderi fell for the first of five times to the

175

The Moghul gate inserted in Babur's gorge.

Delhi and Malwa sultanates, and the great bastions of the Bala Qila are Muslim work. In time Malwa had become independent of Delhi, ruled by its own sultans. The most successful of these was Mahmud Khilji I who reigned for over 30 years, and during his time some of the most notable buildings in the town were made. The Kushak Mahal was built in 1445; only four of its original seven balconied storeys remain, the high walls lit by clerestory windows and vaulted over. The Jami Masjid and the Badal Mahal have the distinctly Persian, pre-Moghul, style of Mandu, with domes and arcades, tapered turrets, eaves and brackets that are especially Gujarati attributes, though these buildings were probably carved by local Hindu craftsmen or those captured in Gujarat.

Babur's occupation was not the end of Chanderi's travails. At least seven times more the fort sustained battles and changed hands between Muslim, Afghan, Rajput and British. The most enduring monuments are the great Jain rock carvings near Babur's breach – three standing figures and three lotus Tirthankaras. Further up the slope, in a cave, are three *murtis*; from here there are stunning views over the lake.

The town of Chanderi, once made rich by the passing of caravans, still has some large *havelis*, merchants' houses, with their distinctive *jali* screens, though most are now whitewashed, with brick-red tiles. Many of the shops are raised on small platforms several feet above ground level, and many of them still sell the sought-after Chanderi saris, as famous as Kashmiri shawls. In very fine weave, in silk and cotton and muslin, these gorgeous cloths are made on antique looms. Bargaining for them among narrow, winding streets in the shadow of ruined caravan-serais and the twilit fortress walls, Chanderi comes vibrantly to life.

Chanderi Fort reflected in the Kirtisagar.

*Chanderi Fort seen beyond Badal
Mahal Gate.*

MANDU

Then said another – 'Surely not in vain
My Substance from the common Earth was ta'en,
That He who subtly wrought me into Shape
Should stamp me back to common Earth again.'

The Rubaiyat of Omar Khayyam
LXI (1st edition) translated by
EDWARD FITZGERALD

The magnificent Mandu city-fortress stands on the crest of the Vindhyas, 1000 feet above the Nimar plains. Shadiabad – City of Joy – the Muslims called it, a place of many palaces mirrored in the lakes and pools of a lush green monsoon land.

The name Mandu derives from the Hindu Mandapa Durg, the Fort of Many Pavilions. There had probably been a fortified settlement here since the 6th century but when the Paramara kings moved their capital from Ujjain to Dhar, about 20 miles away, Mandu became a favoured retreat, even though deep in dangerous tiger country. Raja Bhoj, one of the greatest Hindu kings, built here, centred on the Munja Talao where Sanskrit inscriptions and the remains of Hindu temples can be seen. The Ram Pol, a gateway to the north-east of the city, is believed also to date from the Paramara period.

Mandu's plateau covers about 20 square miles with deep chasms on

Jahaz Mahal, Ship Palace, surrounded by water.

Jami Masjid seen from the Ashrafi Mahal.

The prayer court of the Jami Masjid.

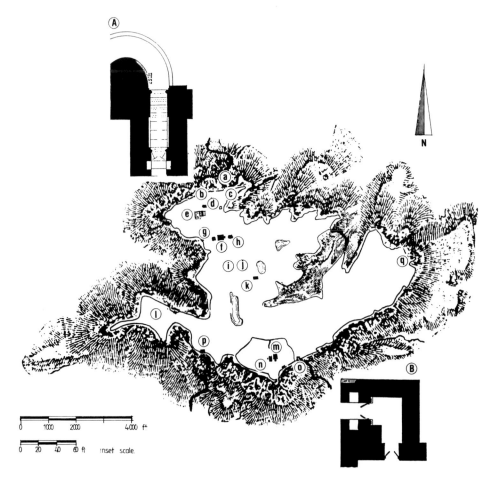

Plan of Mandu:
a. Alamgir Gate
b. Delhi Gate (and inset A)
c. Gadi Gate
d. Hindola Mahal
e. Jahaz Mahal and Munja Tank
f. Jami Masjid
g. Tomb of Hoshang Shah
h. Ashrafi Mahal
i. Mosque of Dilawar Khan
j. Tomb of Darya Khan
k. Mosque of Malik Mughis
l. Songarh
m. Rewa Kund Palace
n. Rupmati's Palace
o. Bhagwania Gate (and inset B)
p. Tarapura Gate
q. Jahangirpur Gate

180

three sides. The strong perimeter wall of rubble and masonry can only have been constructed with great difficulty, following the contours of ravines and passes. The last resort citadel of Bala Qila, at Sonagarh to the west, stands on a virtually isolated upthrust of land that no enemy could storm in strength.

In the aftermath of Timur's invasion of Delhi in 1398, extinguishing the Tughluq dynasty, many of the former Sultan's viceroys proclaimed their independence. In Malwa in 1401 the Governor of Dhar, Dilawar Khan Ghori, who claimed descent from a Damascan royal line, declared himself Sultan of Malwa. The fortifications of Mandu were greatly increased as a result. Two great gates in particular date from this time: a steep ramp sweeps up to the mighty bastion of the Delhi Gate, guarded by several lesser gates; and the ramp of the southern Tarapura Gate is forced through three right-angled turns, a tried and tested defense.

Hoshang Shah succeeded his father and began work on several buildings, including his own tomb, a weighty domed cube relieved only by arched frontispieces, which is among the very earliest Muslim

The white marble tomb of Hoshang Shah.

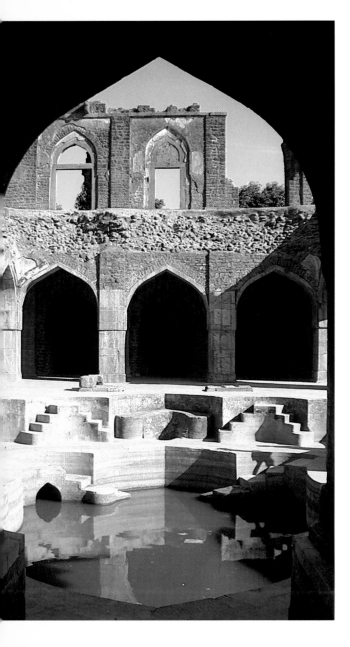

buildings in India to be faced with white marble. Though his father had built several mosques, Hoshang Shah's reign saw the commencement of the great Jami Masjid, perhaps the finest and largest remaining work of Afghan creation in India. Up until then – it was built between 1431 and 1454 – the mosques at Mandu had largely been built with material pillaged from Hindu temples. But the builders of the Jami Masjid dispensed with traditional Hindu structure to create five aisles of 17 domed bays, relying for effect on simple repetition and the play of light over the beautiful red sandstone, sharply delineating the elegant ogee profiles of the arches, and the deep line of shadow thrown by the *chadya*. The dome of the entrance pavilion is echoed by those of the prayer hall and in turn by that of Hoshang Shah's tomb to the west and the Ashrafi Mahal to the east, aligned along the *qibla*. The Persian art of glazing had been carried to Mandu from Multan and flourished here throughout the 15th century: the turquoise blue and radiant yellow tiles of Mandu were unsurpassed, and just sufficient of them remain in the entrance pavilion to demonstrate the skill and artistry of the Malwa craftsmen.

The heavy-set Hindola Mahal was built about 1425, also by Hoshang Shah, possibly as a *durbar* hall: its massive, battered walls with their inclining angle appear to sway slightly, hence the name Swinging Palace. The main hall may have supported more than the present two storeys but it remains one of the finest in India – tremendous arcades round a great room framed with huge transverse ogee arches, and overlooked by a gallery.

Both Hoshang Shah's tomb and the Jami Masjid were completed by his real successor, Mahmud Khan, a Khilji Turk who was minister to Hoshang's son, and poisoned him in 1436. He adopted the style of Mahmud Shah and founded the Khilji dynasty; he proved a fighting ruler, almost always in dispute with his neighbours of Gujarat and Mewar. In particular he clashed with the great Rana Kumbha of Chitor. A disputed victory was claimed by both sides: Rana Kumbha built his nine-storeyed Jayastambha, Tower of Victory, and at Mandu Mahmud made a seven-storeyed tower, which has since collapsed. The base for the tower was provided by a corner pavilion of the Ashrafi Mahal; less solidly constructed than the buildings of Hoshang Shah's day, the palace was striking principally for its brilliant tilework.

Equally colourful was Mahmud's Jahaz Mahal, Ship Palace, built for his queens: three airy halls with a beautiful bathing courtyard, spacious terraces, delicious fountain courts, pavilions, kiosks and cupolas, a magical place reflected in the waters of the Munja and Kapur tanks to either side.

The Khilji dynasty lasted for nearly 100 years. By the early 16th century, Rajputs had risen to dominate the administration, particularly

Jahaz Mahal, Ship Palace, and (opposite) fountain courtyard.

Mahmud II's minister, Medini Rao. Mahmud therefore sought the help of Gujarat's Sultan, and Medini Rao that of Rana Sanga of Mewar. In the following battle Mahmud was beaten but allowed to keep his throne. He made the mistake later of sheltering the rebel brother of the next Sultan of Gujarat, Bahadur Shah, and with his new defeat Mandu was annexed and remained with Gujarat until they both fell to Humayun in 1534. Sher Shah's reign followed but by the time of Humayun's return to power in 1555, the governorship conferred by Sher Shah had become independent, and hereditary.

Baz Bahadur was the last Sultan of Malwa, most famous for his legendary love affair with the beautiful Hindu Rupmati, the lady of the lotus. The romantic Rewa Kund palaces, with their superb views across the Narbada valley far below, held all he asked of life. This idyllic existence came to an abrupt end when the armies of Akbar, hastened by the disaffection of the Afghan nobles, took Mandu in the early 1560s. Baz Bahadur fled the field and Rupmati took poison rather than fall into the hands of Adham Khan, the Moghul general. For the excesses of his sack of Mandu, as well as later crimes, Akbar had Adham Khan thrown from the battlements of Agra Fort.

Akbar and his successors several times used Mandu as a staging post

*Ogee arcades in the Jami Masjid and
Hindola Mahal.*

to the Deccan. Both he and Jehangir attempted to restore some of the
earlier and decaying buildings but their historian, Firishta, recorded
its fortifications as still 'the most extraordinary in the known world'.

In 1732 the Marathas, under Malhar Rao Holkar, defeated the
Moghul governor of Malwa. Eventually an imperial grant from Delhi
confirmed Malwa, and Mandu, as a Maratha holding, and so it remained
until the advent of the British.

Sir Thomas Roe, ambassador of James I, was possibly the first

Englishman to set foot in Mandu, entering as part of Jehangir's train, a triumphal procession of 500 elephants. Roe was lodged in a deserted mosque, and witnessed the Emperor's birthday ceremonies: Jehangir, laden with diamonds, rubies and pearls, was weighed on golden scales in silver, precious stones and cloth of gold, afterwards showering his court with 'nuts and almonds, fruits and spices, all made of thin silver'. Mandu stands today a monument to the transience of such lustre, but unalterably alluring in its promise of glory.

The royal palace reflected in the
Munja Tank.

DAULATABAD

The great granite outcrops of the Deccan are, according to legend, the lumber left discarded after the creation of the world. From the fortresses built on them a succession of dynasties controlled this troublesome region, and with Daulatabad in particular some of the bloodiest events of those reigns are associated.

Deogiri, as the place was first called, had been a Buddhist monastic settlement but the first fort here was probably founded in the 9th century. By the end of the 12th it was an important stronghold of the Yadava kings; poets and a college of astronomy prospered at their courts, and their kingdom extended from the river Krishna to the Narbada.

All the major features of the citadel date from the Yadava period. Its rock, about 200 feet high, was scarped all round to a height of 150 feet, prompting Shahjahan's chronicler to note 'that neither ant nor snake could scale it'. After passing through a hornwork with three gates inside it, leading into and out of the innermost town enclosure containing the ruins of the Yadava palace, the sole entrance to the stronghold opens from a wall walk skirting a huge bastion, and a causeway crossing the moat between descending and ascending flights of steps. The moat had an intricate system of dams, so that the causeway could be flooded. Having negotiated that, any assault would then have to pass through a cavernous L-shaped guard chamber and eventually a dark tortuous tunnel, barred by retractable stone slabs and sealed with an iron trap door that could be fired red-hot; further along, the tunnel became a ventilated chamber which could be filled with smoke to asphyxiate attackers.

In the early 14th century occurred the first contact between the Hindu Deccan and Muslim Delhi. Ala-ud-din Khilji, yet to succeed to the sultanate, carried off an amazing exploit by force-marching through central India at the head of a few thousand cavalry in a bid to capture the rumoured wealth of Deogiri. The Raja, Ramchandra Deva, was beaten into the citadel and beseiged. Ala-ud-din plundered the town at will and was bought off from further tortures with gold, elephants and horses. Preparing for the journey back through land made doubly hazardous by hostile Hindu kings, provoked by his assault on Deogiri yet equally interested in his booty, Ala-ud-din was attacked by the forces of the defeated Raja's son. It was an ill-advised act. 'If my son, in the way of folly and the pride of youth, exalted the spear of valour and hostility, let not your resentment be kindled against me for his rashness.' Understandably, avarice was kindled instead. Ala-ud-din successfully returned to Delhi richer by more than six tonnes of gold, 12 tonnes of silver, about 400 pounds of pearl, 50 pounds of diamonds, emeralds and rubies, thousands of pieces of silk, 50 elephants and 1000 horses.

Ala-ud-din murdered to become Sultan; murder and depravity there-

Daulatabad's celebrated Qila Shikan, Fort Breaker, on its gun emplacement in the citadel commanding the Chand Minar, Victory Tower, and the town below.

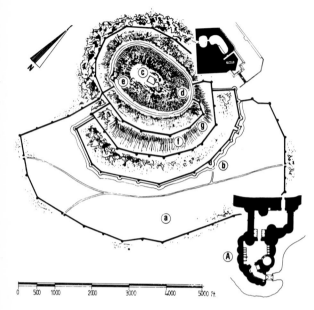

after marred his reign and still more those of his successors. Deogiri had given refuge to the Gujarati king and his daughter Devala Devi: his wife, Kamala Devi, and a young eunuch, Malik Kafur, had already been made prizes of the Sultan. Kafur became a general and, lured by the thought of riches, he made several profitable raids into the Deccan. On one of them he compelled Ramchandra Deva of Deogiri to become Delhi's vassal and the girl, Devala Devi, was married to Khizir Khan in Delhi.

In 1312, when Ramchandra died, Deogiri was annexed and in 1316 Ala-ud-din died, some say with the help of his favourite, Kafur. Certain it is that most of the Sultan's family were imprisoned, killed or blinded, but after 35 days the Sultan's third son, Mubarak, arranged for Kafur's murder – and for those of his surviving brothers – and became Sultan, taking Devala Devi to himself and an outcast *parwari*, Hasan, whom he ennobled as Khusru Khan.

Plan of Daulatabad:
a. Outer town
b. Triple Gate
c. Citadel (with *baradari*)
d. Tunnel
e. Rock temple and moat
f. Jami Masjid
g. Chand Minar

190

Harpal Deva of Deogiri rebelled, was defeated and flayed alive in 1318. Later Mubarak's viceroy in Deogiri rebelled too. The Sultan roused himself once more, horribly punishing the man, returning then to Delhi and to worse excesses. Eventually he was murdered by Khusru Khan, his favourite. Devala Devi was taken by Khusru but heard of no more when the Turkish Ghazi Malik beheaded him and was elected to the throne, becoming, as Tughluq Shah, founder of a new dynasty.

In 1325 he was murdered by his elder son, Muhammad, whose ruthless tyranny, acts of oppression and atrocity need not be recorded, save that in 1327 Muhammad decided to move his capital from Delhi to Deogiri, which would be renamed Daulatabad and would perhaps prove a better base from which to control an empire that now included so much of the south. The move, over 700 miles along a new road, of all the army, nobles, officials and necessary sections of Delhi's common populace, was desperately impractical. The court returned north but not before many had perished or suffered harrowing exaction of taxes to pay for the double journey. Famine compounded the abject state of his subjects: while Muhammad fed his elephants on sugars and rice the people starved, and ate their dead. Undeterred by the wholesale misery inflicted by his absolute power, Muhammad pursued his course with manic intensity.

His governor in Daulatabad, Zafar Khan, rebelled and proclaimed the

LEFT *The Daulatabad hill fort showing the citadel and outer curtain wall with the Chand Minar.*

RIGHT *The fort's defences.*

independent Bahmani kingdom. His capital later moved to Gulbarga and when, at the end of the 15th century, the Bahmani Sultanate disintegrated, Daulatabad became part of the kingdom of Malik Ahmad, founder of the Nizam Shahi dynasty who ruled from Ahmadnagar. Most of Ahmadnagar fell to Akbar in 1600 but Daulatabad remained independent under an Abyssinian slave, Malik Ambar, who rallied Bijapur and Golconda against the Moghuls, and greatly fortified the town.

Of the town's four main ring walls, probably the outer one was built by the Muslims, and they were almost certainly also responsible for strengthening the bastioned gates of the outer walls. The powerful double-walled, double-moated second circuit contains an extraordinary triple gate resembling the great *donjon* of Château Gaillard in France, built by Richard I after crusading against the Muslims in the Holy Land. Most of the ruined mosques and palaces date from the Tughluq and early Bahmani periods, but the earliest mosque was probably made for Mubarak Khilji from material once part of a Hindu temple. The most distinctive landmark of the fort is the pink Chand Minar, Pillar of Victory, which was built in 1435 by one of the Bahmani Sultans, near Muhammad Tughluq's Jami Masjid.

Malik Ambar's son, Fateh Shah, having captured and slain the Nizam

The bronze ram's head of the Qila Shikan elaborately inscribed in Persian, Creator of Storms.

192

Shah of Ahmadnagar, was ready to come to terms with Shahjahan but was persuaded by Bijapur to continue resistance. The Moghul general, Mahabat Khan, determined on taking Daulatabad by assault, something never before achieved. Eventually Fateh Shah sued for peace and was liberally pensioned off, but the young king he had set up was sent to lifelong imprisonment at Gwalior.

Shahjahan dreamed of including in his empire all the lands of his forefathers, including Transoxiana and its capital, Samarkand. His son Aurangzeb, having already been governor of the Deccan and won some victories in Balkh and Badakshan, was forced to retreat before the Uzbeks in 1647, and twice failed, to his elder brother's once, to take the city of Qandahar. He was sent back to the Deccan and took up residence in Daulatabad. In the mid-18th century, after Aurangzeb's death and the rise of the Nizam, Daulatabad was taken by Hyderabad, ceded to the Marathas in 1760 and then regained after their defeat at Panipat in 1761.

The fort is still an impressive presence on its hill: today the most graphic evidence of Daulatabad's fearsome past are the great cannon in their batteries – Qila Shikan, Fort Breaker, and, inscribed in Persian, Creator of Storms. They are things of beauty as well as destruction, somehow symbolising the rich prizes, so sought-after, of the Deccan.

The conical tower guarding the second main entrance in the double walls of the fort.

The moat and water supply at the entrance to the citadel.

193

THE MARATHA FORTS

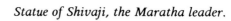
Statue of Shivaji, the Maratha leader.

The natural defences of the Western Ghats, and the panorama from the summit of Rajgad.

195

The Marathas – their name returns like a defiant echo to any proclamation of imperial title to India, reverberating round their strongholds in the Western Ghats for nearly 200 years as they warred with the Moghuls, never wholly conquering, never wholly vanquished. Not until early in the 19th century did dissension in their own ranks and a third war with the British finally destroy their power.

The Marathas were moulded into a real force, almost into a separate nation, by one man, Shivaji Bhonsla, born at Shivneri in 1627. His father and grandfather had been *jaghirs* of the Nizam Shahi Sultan of Ahmadnagar and later of the Adil Shahi Sultan of Bijapur, with several forts in the Poona district under their command. Shivneri itself, and the Junna fort nearby, were garrisoned by the Moghuls in the 1630s in the course of Aurangzeb's policy, as governor of the Deccan for his father the Emperor Shahjahan, to annexe the independent sultanates, of which Bijapur was one. In this way in 1626 the Moghuls had already acquired Purandar which, along with Sinhgad, guarded the route to Poona, itself a *jaghir* that had been given to Maloji, Shivaji's grand-father, in 1604 by the Ahmadnagar Sultan.

Standing at 4000 feet above sea level, the Purandar citadel had re-putedly been built by Purandara or Lord Indra, king of the gods. It is a double *giri durg*, hill fort, with a lower fort, Vajragad, to the east. Unlike some of their Rajput counterparts, the Marathas carefully chose positions which could not be overlooked by adjoining hills, even to the extent of levelling the surrounding ridges by blastworks. Like any other hill fort, Purandar was defended by curtain walls, 26 miles in circuit, with six bastions to guard the three main gates reached by a steep, misty cliff path, often through thick shrubby terrain.

Ten years after they had squeezed Purandar from Bijapur and thus from the holding of the Maratha Bhonslas, the Moghuls similarly acquired Sinhgad, a fort so extraordinarily situated it might seem it could never be taken by force. A long steep climb reveals the fort backed up to massive, rugged mountains on the north and south, with narrow, precipitous ridges to the east and west. Two winding, rocky paths are each defended by three gates; having forced the ascent, beseigers came face to face with a craggy escarpment topped by stone walls.

By the time he was 19, Shivaji was well of an age to avenge the in-justice, as he saw it, done to his father and grandfather by the Moghuls in depriving them of their *swarajya* or homeland, and he began with the capture by bribery of the fort at Torna. With the treasure he won there, Shivaji set about building the fort that would become the capital of Maharashtra, Raigad; before its completion he had also by devious means retaken Sinhgad and Purandar.

Shivaji built over 100 forts. This work, the wars he waged and the armies he maintained were costly affairs, and in order to finance and achieve supremacy over the Moghuls, Shivaji initiated a system of revenues and administration that in his day bore hard on the Marathas' enemies and later, when the Marathas were split into rival groups, also proved a bitter burden on their own people. These 'land Vikings' exacted a payment, the famous Maratha *chauth*, of one quarter of the revenue assessment of any land they could dominate. Where they could not dominate they plundered in fierce combined attacks of

196

cavalry and infantry. In 1657 Shivaji made a night attack on Junna during its Moghul occupation and successfully made off with considerable booty, including 200 horses. That year he also attempted to win back his birthplace, Shivneri, but was beaten off: its rough, steep path is guarded by seven gates with bastions, and battlemented walls.

Seven years later Shivaji made two attacks which brought down on him and his people the protracted vengeance of Aurangzeb, who by now had emerged victorious from the imperial wars of succession, and was Emperor. His determination to win the Deccan would in any case have entailed conflict with the Marathas, but this was precipitated in 1664 when Shivaji sacked the Moghul seaport of Surat, with its rich factories or trading stations belonging to Dutch, British and French merchants. The Europeans put up stiff resistance and a large part of the town escaped damage or looting, though the population suffered cruelly: those who were captured and refused to reveal the whereabouts of their treasury had the information extracted by hideous mutilations before death. Several months earlier, Shivaji had raided Poona, snaring Shayasta Khan, the Moghul viceroy, in his harem, and inflicting many casualties. The viceroy escaped and was recalled in ignominy, but was later appointed viceroy of Bengal.

Aurangzeb intended to punish Shivaji's effrontery and the following year sent his Rajput general, Jai Singh of Amber, to beseige the Maratha chieftain at Purandar, about 20 miles from Poona. In fact, it was the very presence of the defensive Vajragad that proved Purandar's undoing, commanding as it did one of the outer fortifications of the upper fort. The Moghul army captured Vajragad, then, building siege towers

Shivneri, the birthplace of Shivaji.

197

The three-pronged shape of Rajgad.

*Rajgad: the purely defensive
Sanjivini Terrace.*

198

to mount their heavy guns, they raked the principal defences. Even *Purandar Fort.*
though his artillery hammered back strike for strike and the outcome
of the battle looked by no means a certain Moghul victory, Shivaji
decided to come to terms. He ceded 23 forts, including Sinhgad, retain-
ing only 12 forts as the Maratha homeland. In 1667, Aurangzeb conferred the title Raja on his erstwhile enemy.

It was not to be expected that Shivaji would remain long under the
Moghul yoke. With his storm troops he re-took a number of the forts he
had relinquished by the treaty of Purandar, and sacked Surat a second
time. In 1670 the Marathas proved their fighting mettle, if proof were
needed, by the astonishing feat of capturing Sinhgad in a 'death or
glory' escalade. After a siege of less than a week, the Marathas assaulted
the high, smooth escarpment in a terrifying rush, forming human
ladders to reach the walls and battlements. In fierce hand-to-hand com-
bat, the Maratha general Tanaji Malusara and the Rajput fort commander

Udaibhan were both killed. This was a great victory for the Marathas. Their daring and valour against a brave defence are remembered in minstrels' ballads, and the tomb of Tanaji is revered not just by his own people but by all those who place a value on soldierly virtues. It is, without doubt, for the martial exploits it engendered that Sinhgad is spoken of, and visited, today.

In 1670 Shivaji made another attempt to wrest Shivneri from the Moghuls, but failed. Nevertheless, his people regarded him with a special mixture of awe and love, and his enthronement in 1670 at Raigad as Chattrapati – Lord of the Umbrella, a godlike appellation – affirmed the greatness of his power: through him their identity was fixed, their place to a great extent assured. On his appearance at the ceremony with the queen consort Soyra, his assembled court and warriors would cry: 'Our dignified king, like Indra the King of Gods, takes his seat on the Umbrella Throne: Born of the fighting race, his

name is Shivaji the King: May he be victorious!'

One of the great merits of Shivaji was the way in which he largely demolished the divisive system of caste that so narrowly ordained Brahman supremacy in other Hindu kingdoms. To be accepted as leader Shivaji had originally been obliged to seek a Brahman proclamation that he was Suryavanshi, a descendant of the sun, and therefore deemed fit to rule. In fact he was a Sudra: low-born like the majority of the Maratha people, he was one of the *kunbi* or cultivator caste. The other great Maratha chiefs who came to prominence from this time were also Sudras: Scindia was a *kunbi*, Gaekwad was of the *gauli* or cowherd caste, and Holkar was of the *dhangar* or shepherd caste. It was not until the mid-18th century that caste jealousies between the chiefs and the Brahman Peshwas, hereditary prime ministers of the Marathas, broke the mould of the Maratha nation that had been Shivaji's outstanding creation.

His military and civil organisations were simple and worked well. The infantry was built up in three graded units of 10, and the cavalry in three graded units of 25 with an overall commander; the cavalry were either state-mounted or had their own horses. There were no hereditary *jaghirs* and the fort garrisons were carefully monitored: no camp women were allowed; accounting was handled by Brahmans; and Shivaji personally inspected the forts, either in the idle, rainy season or on campaign, from October to April. Each fort was well provided with water, oil and grain, and was equipped with a body of men to provide all the skills necessary to a standing army – gunsmiths, blacksmiths, stableboys, swordsmiths and armourers.

Shivaji's civil administration was in a sense an extension of the army, as it was dependent upon the effectiveness of the militia in imposing blackmail payments of *chauth* rather than mere spasmodic plunder; sometimes an extra payment, *sandeshmukhi*, was demanded, the ruler's direct perquisite. That such a system, based for the most part on compulsion, could be established and maintained points to a corresponding fundamental weakness in the Moghul administration of the Deccan. As Raja, Shivaji had appointed eight ministers, each dealing with a specific brief, rather as a cabinet minister would have, of whom the senior was the Peshwa, the prime minister.

On the road to Rajgad from Poona is a memorial pillar showing Shivaji being visited by the goddess Tulaja Bhavani, who had given him a sword, the Bhavani sword, before an important battle, and also showing his seal. A Sanskrit inscription on the pillar declares: 'The Kingdom of Shivaji will be ever-increasing like a crescent moon, and this seal belongs to the son of Shivaji.'

Shivaji had built his capital, Raigad, with treasure won at Torna, and there he had installed his mother, Jiji Bai, a devout and higher caste Hindu than her husband. She had had great influence over her son, instilling in him deference for the Hindu holy things, 'Gods and Cows, Brahmans and the Faith'. Raigad was considered during Shivaji's time to be one of the strongest forts in India, and in 1978 at a Fort Exhibition at Lucerne, a model of it was displayed as the best hill fort in the world. There are 1400 steps up to the fort, but for anyone to whom this is too daunting a prospect, the hire of a 'doolie' can be negotiated with the locals. A 'doolie' is a coarsely woven round basket supported on two

Sinhgad: the Kalyan Gate.

long poles, carried by four bearers, who are replaced by other bearers along the ascent. It is a long and precarious climb and has to be made at sunset, when the heat of the day has lessened, so darkness has fallen by the time the summit is reached. A visit to Raigad necessarily includes an overnight stay at the small rest house there, primitive but clean, with cooking done over an open fire, an experience which adds greatly to the sense of adventure in discovering these rarely visited but most interesting forts: they are a clear object lesson in the whys and wherefores of this period of Indian history.

The main gate, the Maha Darwaza, is flanked by two vast bastions, both over 70 feet high, one convex, the other concave. There are three lines of fortification and many tanks, including the very large Ganga Sagar and one shaped like a crescent moon. Among several wide terraces lies Shivaji's palace and, nearby, the ruins of eight houses where his eight ministers stayed; in the courtyard is a low platform where the throne of the Chattrapati stood. The Jagadishwara Temple has a Nandi bull outside and an inscription to Hanuman, the Monkey God, inside; close by is the *samadhi* of Shivaji and a chattri for his faithful dog. From Takmak Point, the Maha Darwaza can be seen with a large, empty tank nearby; this, the Hathi Talar, is where the elephants used to splash and wallow. One of the most interesting sights is the marketplace with two rows of more than 40 shops: 2000 people lived at Raigad as court, garrison and commissariat. A zigzag road leads from Raigad to another fort, Pratapgad, interesting for its statue of Shivaji and a temple dedicated to Tulaja Bhavani with a pair of *dipmal*, lantern

Purandar Fort.

A Nandi pavilion in the Kedarashwar Temple (left) and a statue of Murar Baji, a fighting general in Shivaji's army.

ABOVE *Pratapgad: steps leading to the main gate and one of a pair of dipmal, lantern pillars, at the Bhavani Temple.*

Sinhgad: the first and second Poona Gates and a crude relief depicting human sacrifice on the founding of the fort.

pillars, that were a special feature in Maharashtra.

In 1675 Shivaji made yet another attack on Shivneri but still that prize eluded him; he died in 1680 of dysentery, aged only 53. Had he lived as long as Aurangzeb, had he come to a better understanding of the British, the history of India over the next two centuries might well have been different.

A son of Shivaji, Shambhuji, succeeded him but almost at once rivalries within the ruling clan brought about a weakening of their power and a reduction in their territory, since Aurangzeb had now embarked on a sustained campaign to break the confederacy. Shambhuji was captured by the Emperor in 1689 and, having refused all terms, was, with his ministers, put to a lingering death. His son Shahu was spared and brought up at the Moghul court, while Raja Ram, another son of Shivaji, was crowned and promptly besieged by the Moghuls at Raigad. He escaped in the guise of a mendicant and after a seven-month siege the fort fell; great treasure and the golden throne of Shivaji were part of the Moghuls' prize but the fort itself they gave into the keeping of the Abyssinian Sidhis of Janjira.

Raja Ram moved his government to Gingee and after his death in 1700 his widow, Tara Bai, acted as regent from Satara. Between 1699

and 1703 Aurangzeb captured at least eight Maratha forts, including Sinhgad, Torna, Raigad and Satara, but most of these were taken by bribery and with no real strength behind their occupation they were often recaptured by the Marathas. Sinhgad was retaken in 1705, during the monsoon.

Aurangzeb died in 1707 and Shahu returned to his people. In 1719, 16,000 Maratha cavalry accompanied the defeated viceroy of the Deccan to Delhi to demand their rights to *swarajya*, *chauth* and *sandeshmukhi*, and they returned in triumph to Satara. Shahu reigned till 1749, a reign that saw the establishment of the Peshwa as an hereditary office. The first to hold this was Balaji Vishvanath Bhat, who had been so effective at Delhi; his son Baji Rao I procured Malwa outright and a holding in Gujarat. It was during this period that the four main Maratha chiefs and their clans – Holkar, Scindia, Gaekwad and Bhonsla – became strongly defined in power and in territory: Holkar and Scindia in Malwa, Gaekwad in Gujarat and Bhonsla in Berar, a confederacy headed now by the Peshwas. The Maratha star began to wane and in 1761 they were disastrously beaten at Panipat by the Afghan Ahmad Shah Abdali.

In 1772, on the death of a new young Peshwa, Madha Rao I, and for the next 30 years, the five Maratha powers became increasingly independent of each other and, as the five Deccani sultanates had done,

The fortified terraces of Pratapgad with Abdullah's Tower (right).

Raigad: the Maha Darwaza, main gate, convex and concave bastions reached by 1400 steps and (right) *the high curtain walls that snake above the gorge defending the fort's north-west approach, seen from Takmak Point.*

they came in time to prey on each other, sometimes in league with one or other clan against a third but invariably bringing hardship and want upon the people held in their dominion, and entirely dissipating the unity of *swarajya* and of purpose that had made them, under Shivaji, the heirs apparent to the Moghul Empire.

The British now began to play a strong part in Maratha affairs, if at first confusingly. In 1775 the Peshwa Raghunath had eventually felt constrained to ask for British help in maintaining his own position and the Company's Bombay Council gave that help by the treaty of Surat. The Calcutta Council objected and reversed this action in 1776 by a new treaty of Purandar; but in 1778 London ordered the Governor of Bengal, Warren Hastings, to reinstate the earlier support of Raghunath. This was the start of the first Maratha war and in 1779 the British were heavily defeated at Wadgaon. The war was ended in 1782 by the treaty of Salbai, with almost no appreciable change in the situation of 1775 except for the debilitating effect of nearly eight years of war. The British were disorganised: they were at war in North America, with France and Spain hostile, and in India there was war from 1780 with Mysore under Haidar Ali. By the treaty of Mangalore made with his successor, Tipu Sultan, they gained some peace but, more importantly, the realisation that they had in India at least withstood two powerful confederacies – without gain perhaps, but without giving ground.

Almost at once the Marathas erupted into conflict among themselves. In 1802 at the Battle of Poona, Jaswant Rao Holkar beat Daulat Rao Scindia and the new Peshwa, Baji Rao II, who sought the help of the Governor-General, Wellesley, by the treaty of Bassein. Holkar then withdrew, leaving the Bhonsla Raja of Berar and Scindia to fight the second Maratha war with the British and the Peshwa, Gaekwad having remained neutral. Wellesley in 1803 at Assaye and Argaon, with Lake at Delhi and Aligarh, and Laswara at Scindia, broke the power of the Bhonsla Raja and Scindia, achieving great gains in land. Holkar, however, remained hostile and undefeated, and Wellesley was recalled.

The Marathas were almost bankrupted by war and the British were distracted by Napoleon's successful wars in Russia and their own efforts to counter increasing French power in the East Indies. Into the resultant vacuum two new forces rose to terrorise India – the Pathans under Amir Khan but nominally serving Holkar, and the Pindaris, the *pendhara* freebooters who had attached themselves in the past to the Maratha armies. These wide-ranging groups of cavalry, especially the Pindaris, hit hard and indiscriminately, mustering and dispersing freely and fast, with no fixed base where they could be attacked. Hastings returned to India and by 1817 was ready to put his plan – to isolate the Maratha powers and eradicate the Pathan and Pindari menace – into operation; and with 14 divisions campaigning almost as independent armies, he succeeded. Though the deposed Peshwa's son, Nana Sahib, lived to fulminate on his wrongs and strike again at the British in the Mutiny massacre at Cawnpore in 1857, for the time being, through outright defeat or by treaty, the British achieved supremacy in India. Amongst other victories they took the Maratha forts of Raigad, Purandar and Sinhgad, from where, in triumph, they carried off Shivaji's Bhavani sword.

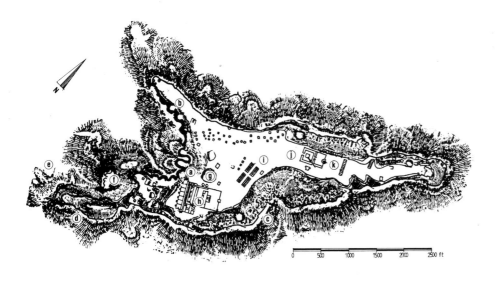

Plan of Raigad :
a. Maha Darwaza
b. Chor Dindi
c. Wagh Gate
d. Khubladha
e. Wadi
f. Nana Gate
g. Ganga Sagar
h. Citadel Palace
i. Bazaar
j. Jagwishwara Temple
k. Shivaji's *samadhi*

211

GULBARGA

An iron fist in an iron land: such was Gulbarga, stronghold of the Bahmani kings. The kingdom was born in rebellion and continued in strife while it existed, embattled with Delhi, with the Hindu kingdoms of Vijayanagar and Warangal, and in dynastic murder.

In 1347 the Turki or Afghan, Zafar Khan, Governor of Daulatabad for Muhammad bin Tughluq, declared his independence; announcing descent from a Persian king, Bahman, who was perhaps Artaxerxes, he took the turquoise throne as Ala-ud-din Hasan Shah al-wali al Bahmani. The capital was moved here from Daulatabad; and although Bahmani history is as bloody and barbarous as any of the period, its buildings held a unique place in all India.

Amid the desolation of the fort one may read the immensity of strength and sophistication of military engineering that was Gulbarga. It was a *nara durg* with no natural defences. Instead, a 50-foot thick double wall was surrounded by a wide moat, scraped out of rock, with a drawbridge and postern on the eastern side; the wall walk of the inner range rose high above the outer one to provide formidable two-tier defences. The really massive projecting bastions held revolving platforms for cannon; there were machicolations, merlons and embrasures with loopholes for musketry. The western gate is a spectacular horn-shaped projection incorporating four gates and four guarded courts to deflect attackers beneath the fire of battlements and bastions. The doors between the pair of outer bastions had four-pronged spikes to prevent battering by elephants; three sets of iron chains and heavy wooden bars could be thrown across them for extra defence.

The outer curtain walls and Jami Masjid of Gulbarga Fort viewed from across the lake.

Sunset over Gulbarga.

213

Alone among Indian Forts, Gulbarga boasted a huge, grim *donjon*, the Bala Hissar keep in the centre of the fort, used as a residence and place of last refuge. Rectangular, with four great towers, its grey-black sandstone walls are unrelieved by any openings below the level of the crenellations except the entrance, high up on the north face at the head of a long, exposed flight of steps. There is no doubt that the builders of Gulbarga had journeyed far afield or had travelled thence to the

A tongawallah washes down his horse in the moat below the double walls of Gulbarga.

Deccan: the fort is clearly marked by knowledge of the Frankish castles of the Crusaders, like Krak des Chevaliers, or Aleppo of the Seljuks.

In the wake of Muhammad bin Tughluq's transferral of his capital to Daulatabad came skilled artisans, bringing to the Deccan the building styles of Delhi, and of Persia. Gulbarga's Jami Masjid, built in 1367 by Rafi of Kazvin, is unique in India in that it is completely covered, with a dome over the *mihrab*, domes at each corner and more than 70 smaller

Bala Hissar or keep.

domes. There is no open courtyard – all light comes from the arcades. The entire visual effect is drawn from the repetition of arches, ogee and cusped, and the trefoil form used in the great central prayer hall, recalling the Jami Masjids of Herat and Isfahan.

The tombs of the early Bahmani kings are simple domed cubes of plastered rubble in northern style, but the mausoleum of Firoz Shah does bear some Hindu decoration, though this remained uncommon in the Deccan until the time of the Adil Shahi dynasty towards the end of the 15th century.

Ala-ud-din Bahmani died in 1358; by then his considerable domains included the port of Goa on the western coast. His successor, Muhammad I, waged savage wars with Vijayanagar and Warangal. According to the historian Firishta, in 1365 the Bahmanis used gunpowder against Vijayanagar nearly 200 years before Babur introduced it into northern India. It is said that the Bahmani artillery was commanded by Venetians and Ottoman Turks, and that this one battle claimed half a million Hindu slain. After it, the warring sides agreed to spare the lives of non-combatants in future battles.

Muhammad was equally ruthless with the robbers in his own land, most probably peasants driven by desperation to brigandage. Twenty thousand were recorded killed on his orders. He ceaselessly patrolled his kingdom, further enforcing his mastery by crushing currency reforms: all Hindu coins were banned and all Hindu goldsmiths and moneychangers executed.

The Bahmani kings were harsh and dissolute without exception, but the havoc they wrought in wars and massacres was at least matched by their depredations on their own flesh and blood: the eighth king, in 1397, Firoz Shah, was no further removed than nephew from Muhammad I. His reign saw the creation of many public buildings and palaces, and a thriving bazaar stemming from trade between the kingdom's ports and Persia, Africa and Mediterranean Europe. He, too, perpetrated massacres at Vijayanagar in 1406 but afterwards took a Vijayanagar princess to wife and restored the right of banking to Hindu goldsmiths. However in 1420 he was defeated at Pangal, north of the Krishna river, and two years later was murdered by his brother Ahmad, who subsequently moved his capital to Bidar.

The reigns of Ahmad and his successors were little better than those that had gone before – dreadful deeds of war and bigotry, against Hindus, between the Deccani Sunni Muslims and Shi'ite Turks and Persians. Gulbarga was razed to the ground in 1520 by the Vijayanagar king Krishna Deva Raya. With the end of the reign of Mahmud Shah came the end of the Bahmani kingdom. The governors of its provinces set up their own sultanates – Berar, Ahmadnagar, Bijapur, Bidar and Golconda – which lasted until Aurangzeb annexed them into his empire. Gulbarga itself fell to him in 1657.

It is the smaller exploits of man that have survived here. Uniquely in this fort stands a double row of caravanserai houses, unchanged and undamaged since they were built. Each has a similar pointed arch doorway onto the dusty street between them, leading to the western gate. Brilliantly white-washed, they are lived and worked in by Muslim families, trading prosperously, and in peace.

The Jami Masjid entrance portal and outer arcade.

217

BIDAR

Gumbad Darwaza, the main gate, and bridge over the triple moat.

The Madrasa of Mahmud Gawan faced with Persian ceramic tiles.

The grace and symmetry of Bidar shimmer like a mirage, an exquisite Persian city transported to the harsh Deccani country. Domes, minarets, arches, balustrades and spacious gardens flowing with water – all express that distinctive style in colours synonymous with Persia, brilliant turquoise blue and gorgeous sunflower yellow.

The fort walls are six miles round, the buildings within so many and so enticing it seems one might never get to the end of exploring them. Through arches to roofless pavilions, down long, narrow, vaulted passages, up and down steep steps to yet another palace, past mosques to fountained pools, by a fine triple-arched gate to ever more halls of audience.

The Chaubara, watchtower, at the crossing of the town's two main streets.

The domed roof and prayer gall arcades of the Sola Kumbha Masjid.

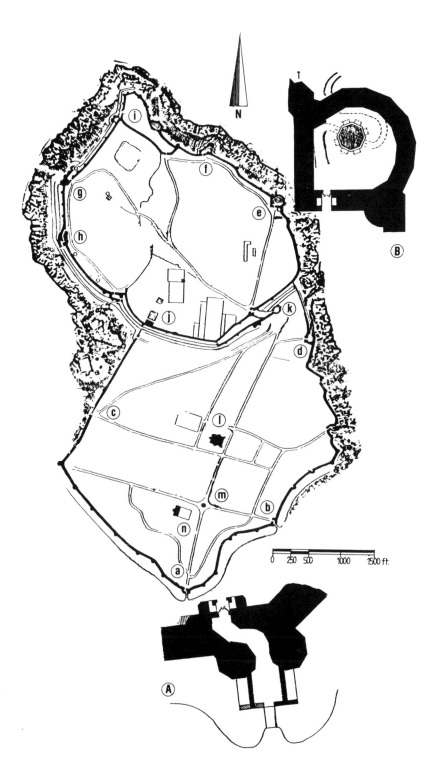

Plan of Bidar:
a. Fateh Gate (and insert A)
b. Mangalpet Gate
c. Shahgarij Gate
d. Talghat Gate
e. Mandu Gate (and inset B)
f. Kalmadgi Gate
g. Delhi Gate
h. Kalyani Gate
i. Citadel
j. Palaces and Sola Kumbha Masjid
k. Gumbad Darwaza
l. Madrasah of Mahmud Gawan
m. Chaubara
n. Jami Masjid

221

Such beauty and elegance perhaps seem at variance with the violent and tyrannous dynasties of the period, but there is surely an underlying significance to much of what may be seen. The repeated rhythms of the buildings, the order and harmony of perspectives are charged, consciously or not, with the simple power and inevitability of revealed Islam. The same symmetry of design is found in the formal garden, introduced into India by the Muslims. It was a luxury, a retreat from harsh surrounds for them, a place of green and flowers and scent and water, a kind of Paradise.

The ninth Bahmani king, Ahmad Shah, had moved his capital 60 miles north from Gulbarga to Bidar, as much for its high cool situation as to distance himself from the dangerous Hindu kingdom of Vijayanagar. He had broken the compact earlier made with the Raya not to slay non-combatants, by unexpectedly raiding and massacring Hindus in revenge for his brother's defeat and losses in 1420, destroying temples and colleges as he went. Some Brahmans, however, converted to Islam and held high office for the Bahmanis: one, renamed Fathullah, became Governor of Berar and broke away to be its first independent Sultan; another, renamed Hasan, founded the Nizam Shahi dynasty of Ahmadnagar. The rivalry between such converted Deccanis and 'foreigners' of Persian, Afghan or Turkish origin led to the breakup of the Bahmani kingdom, with 'foreign' governors establishing their own kingdoms at Golconda and Bijapur.

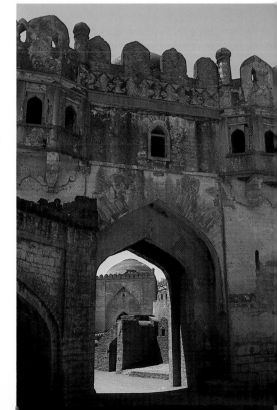

The fort, approached through the town on the southern side, lies at the head of a gradually rising promontory with its citadel at the northern tip, perched over a dramatic 300-foot drop. The town is surrounded by

222

its own curtain wall, moated for much of its length and abutting onto that of the fort, still marvellously preserved. On the town side, where the ground is lowest, the fort's defences are multiple: the impressive triple moat is 30 feet deep and hewn out of solid rock; its system of dams and sluices enabled defenders to isolate the fort at will. The town and fort walls are connected in the east by a dam crossing all three moats, and in the west the central channel cuts the town wall under the protection of the Naubat Khana, where buglers and drummers could sound the alarm.

The walls, bastions, gates and barbicans of Bidar are some of the most sophisticated in India still visible intact. The Munda Burj is the most prominent bastion, commanding the approach with heavy guns, and loopholes and gun-slits in two tiers for marksmen. The town could be entered through five gates, of which the most interesting are the southern Fateh Gate, with squat octagonal towers, drawbridge, barbican and a serpentine passage leading to iron-plated spiked doors; and the elevated Talghat Gate in the east, reached by a steep ramp.

The fort walls on the town side are over 40 feet high, doubled in places and up to 50 feet thick. The main entrance from the town is a triple gate, with vivid blue and turquoise tiles, over the triple moat; the second gate, the Sharzu Darwaza, is decorated with tigers. Of the other five gates into the fort, the most prominent is the barbicaned Delhi Gate; others were protected by precipitous tunnels – that of the Mandu Gate looped through a subterranean guardroom.

The Bahmani kings contributed very little to the progress or well-being of India. One of the four who followed Ahmad Shah was Humayun

The Banjara gypsies, who originated from Bidar and spread throughout the world, still live around the fort.

The double walls of the fort and tilework on the outer gatehouse between the town and the fort.

the Tyrant. One may stop and ponder the ferocity that must have merited such an epithet in a time of such unbridled power to inflict cruelty and suffering. Another was Muhammad Shah III, whose reign was chiefly remarkable for a famine; for the sack of a Hindu centre of learning, Kondapalli, and of Sanchi, one of the seven Hindu sacred cities, with accompanying slaughter; and for an outstanding man who served under him, as he had under Humayun – a Persian scholar, general and administrator, the Khwafa Mahmud Gawan.

He founded in 1472 the great *madrasah* or college, a marvellous three-storeyed building with a monumental minaret, great arches on its axes, arcading and brilliantly coloured chevron tilework. The domes over the main chambers, beyond the arches, were among the first in India to take the characteristically Timurid bulbous form, more frequently used in the 16th century. There are two important mosques here: the extensive Jami Masjid and the Sola Kumbha Masjid – its name means '16 pillars' – with a remarkable dome on a lofty 16-sided drum.

To walk among the ruined palaces of Bidar is truly to walk back to another time. Imposing black granite steps, striking amid the red

sandstone, lead to the Gangan Mahal, a Hall of Public Audience; there are lovely arabesque designs and glazed mosaics in the Rangin Mahal of Ali Barid Shah; the high art of Quranic calligraphy; bright painted murals in the *zenana*; the coolness of gardens like the Lal Bagh by the Takht Mahal or Throne Palace; the 70-foot Chaubara, the watchtower that dominates the centre of the town.

Qasim Barid, the Turkish minister of the last Bahmani king, exercised power in reality and after a series of puppet sultans, his son, Amir Barid Shah, in 1526 assumed rule in his own right and his line continued till about 1619, when Bidar was annexed by Bijapur. The tiled tombs of the Barid Shahis are outside the town walls to the west, and are well preserved.

A dusty road runs round the perimeter of Bidar frequented by bullock carts carrying sugar cane and by the local Banjara tribe, the original gypsy race, colourful figures weighed down by quantities of traditional silver jewellery and *bidri*-work. In the lanes and alleyways of Bidar the artisans of this delicate damascene metalware – silver and gold inlaid on iron – can be watched at work: designer, moulder, inlayer and engraver, using Persian, even Chinese, motifs in ageless artistry.

Arches and arcades of the royal palaces within the fort.

GOLCONDA

Seen across the Deccani plains from Hyderbad, Golconda presents an arresting silhouette, its steeply upthrust labyrinth of minarets and terraces, pavilions, domes and arches glinting like the facets of a huge uncut diamond.

Centuries ago, the city's caravanserais flocked with merchants, travellers, jewellers and thieves, drawn into a shifting, arguing, watchful throng from far and wide across the Orient to covet, barter, sell or steal one thing, the gemstones which made Golconda famous in a land fabled for its wealth. Even after the days of the rapacious Moghuls, the Nizam of Hyderbad was reputedly the richest man in the world, and he kept his diamonds in the fortress here, all except for one, the 160-carat Jacob diamond, used daily as a paperweight.

The sultanate of Golconda was formed in 1518 on the dissolution of the Bahmani kingdom, when its Turki governor declared independence and assumed the title Sultan Quli Qutb Shah. The land had centuries

before belonged to the Hindu kingdom of Warangal – meaning 'solitary rock' and named after one of the fantastically-shaped outcrops of granite and gneiss found all over the Deccan. The Shi'ite Qutb Shahi dynasty was undoubtedly one of the most liberal and cosmopolitan of all India's ruling houses while it lasted. Golconda's traders flourished in security and affluence, Hindus lived peaceably among the Muslims, free to practise their own religion and free to share in government and high office. The reigns of the Qutb Shahis were long, especially by the standard of the times. Perhaps, as everywhere, only the peasantry led lives of unremitting labour, under constant threat of losing what little they had.

Quli Qutb Shah reigned till he was 90 but was then killed, in 1543, at the instigation of his son Jamshid. His reign was brief and in 1550 the title was offered to his brother Ibrahim Qutb Shah, who reigned till 1580. During these years the fort achieved its architectural splen-

Golconda Fort and perimeter walls.

dour and its triple-walled defences were greatly reinforced.

The outer wall girdles the whole town, and the central wall the base of the fortress hill. The inner wall follows the rocky contour of the topmost ridge, almost three miles round and strengthened by 87 bastions, some of them still with heavy engraved cannon in place. Only four of the original eight gateways are in use today. The main entrance is the heavily spiked Fateh Darwaza, Victory Gate, in itself a formidable defence against the battering of war elephants. It also possessed an unexpected protection against surprise attack: a sophisticated echo system effective from this lowest guardhouse to the topmost citadel, so that a shout, a dog barking, a drum or bugle, even a clap of the hands, would carry the alarm to sentinels posted along the route. All the gates – the others are Banjara, Mecca and Jamali – are decorated with reliefs of animals and birds, and Fateh Darwaza also bears the image of a Hindu deity.

Inside the walls are the ruins of temples and mosques, palaces and *zenanas* begun by Quli Qutb Shah and extended by his successors. The citadel, the Bala Hissar, stands 350 feet high and within several tiers of fortifications which today, in parts, resemble an extraordinary avalanche of fallen masonry and enormous granite boulders. Cobbled pathways wind among the roofless Rani Mahal, reached by the King's Steps, the Shila Khana or Armoury, and the Jami Masjid, built during the reign of Quli Qutb, all damaged during the later Moghul sieges.

In 1589 Muhammad Quli Qutb Shah moved his capital a few miles from Golconda to Bhaghagar, the city that is now Hyderabad but said to have been built for and named after Bhagmati, a beautiful Hindu girl

An avalanche of masonry tumbles from the Bala Hissar citadel.

228

A carving of lions overcoming elephants in a frieze on the main gate symbolises Golconda's victories.

A fountain court in the Rani Mahal.

RIGHT *A mosque in the citadel and the tomb of Muhammad Quli Qutb Shah.*

beloved of Muhammad Quli; her *baradari* and a masjid named after her still stand. Muhammad Quli also built the famous Charminar at Bhagnagar, a superb triumphal archway, dating from 1592, with four soaring minarets; it is surely the culmination of the Deccani school of architecture, in its graceful synthesis of Hindu and Persian styles.

Apart from its rivalry with Bijapur, Golconda's only real war had come in 1565 when it joined the confederacy of Bidar, Ahmadnagar and Bijapur against the southern Hindu kingdom of Vijayanagar at the battle of Talikota. By dint of diplomacy and gifts, Golconda kept the Moghuls at bay but while Aurangzeb was governor of the Deccan for his father, the Emperor Shahjahan, he entered into a compact with the treacherous Persian, Mir Jumla. This chief minister for Abdullah Qutb Shah had appropriated what was effectively an independent domain within the sultanate, to keep which he enlisted under Shahjahan. Aurangzeb was determined to annexe all the Deccani sultanates, and captured Hyderabad, the Shah retreating to Golconda. Inexorably, Aurangzeb laid siege to the fort in 1656, rejecting all proposals for peaceful settlement until called off by Shahjahan. The following year the Emperor fell ill and the wars for the succession distracted Aurangzeb from the Deccan. Mir Jumla kept his lands and served the Moghul well, proving a brilliant general during his campaigns in Bengal; he died at Dacca in 1663.

It was not until 1687 that Aurangzeb was free of his struggles with the Marathas and could turn his mind once more to Golconda. Abu-l Hassan Qutb Shah, preferring a life of pleasure, had left affairs of state to his Brahman minister, Madanna, who ten years earlier had entered a personally rewarding defence pact with the Maratha leader, Shivaji. With the Marathas held in check Aurangzeb first re-took Hyderabad, Abu-l Hassan, like Abdullah Qutb Shah before him, fleeing to the nearby hill fort, but unlike him heading a staunch resistance for nine months through summer heat and monsoon downpour against bombardment, mining and infantry assault. Bribery succeeded where force could not and in October 1687 Golconda was taken, despite fighting that carried right up to the Bala Hissar. On the summit today stand the remains of a once lovely *baradari*, offering dramatic views across the countryside.

Abu-l Hassan was exiled to Daulatabad and is the only Qutb Shahi not buried at Golconda. The tombs of the other sultans are to the north-west of the fort. Those of Muhammad Quli Qutb and Abdullah Qutb are perhaps the finest but all have interesting and varied arched interiors; fragments of tilework can still be seen and the black tombs bear inscriptions in several scripts.

Golconda was eventually possessed in 1724 by the Nizam-ul-Mulk, and was once more re-fortified to become the world's most impressive diamond vault.

BIJAPUR

The architectural splendours of Bijapur are without question deserving of the kind of appreciation usually reserved for Delhi and for Agra. It would take days to see everything worthy to be seen in this vast city-fortress, and only the chief among its marvels can be mentioned here. Anyone who visits Bijapur will see some of the very best that India has to offer.

The Adil Shahi dynasty of Bijapur were almost all Shi'ite Muslims and exercised a most tolerant rule over other sects and religions, sharing with Golconda among the Deccani sultanates a liberality and enlightenment unusual anywhere in those times.

The Arh Qila citadel walls from the south-east.

Yusuf Adil, a self-exiled Turk, had served under the Bahmani king at Bidar; in time he became Governor of Bijapur and in 1490 he declared independence from the increasingly degenerate Bahmani rule. Yusuf married the sister of a defeated Maratha chieftain and readily admitted Hindus to high office; the Marathi language was used for all business transactions. He was, according to the historian Muhammad Qasim, better known as Firishta, 'a wise prince, intimately acquainted with human nature'. He was also a musician and well read, encouraging scholars and ambassadors to his courts. He resided mostly in the great concentric fort at Raichur, with its amazing boulder-strewn *motte*, founded in Yadava times; but the cosmopolitan Goa was a favourite place with him until he died in 1510, the year in which the port was lost to the Portuguese, re-taken and then, after Yusuf's death, once more captured by Albuquerque.

The gigantic city walls of Bijapur, over six miles round, were begun by Yusuf and are in a good state of repair, moated and crenellated and strengthened by 100 bastions, all adapted for artillery. The stoutest of these bore really heavy guns. The Burj-i-Sherza, Lion Bastion, so

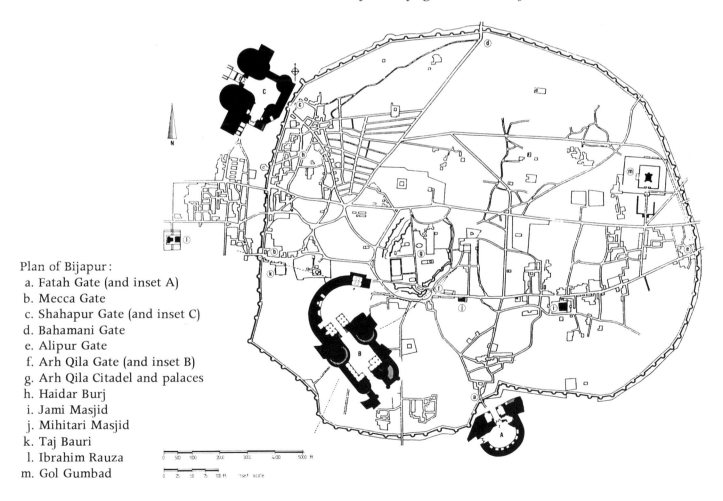

Plan of Bijapur:
 a. Fatah Gate (and inset A)
 b. Mecca Gate
 c. Shahapur Gate (and inset C)
 d. Bahamani Gate
 e. Alipur Gate
 f. Arh Qila Gate (and inset B)
 g. Arh Qila Citadel and palaces
 h. Haidar Burj
 i. Jami Masjid
 j. Mihitari Masjid
 k. Taj Bauri
 l. Ibrahim Rauza
 m. Gol Gumbad

named for the two stone lion heads carved in it, holds the Malik-i-Maidan, Lord of the Battle Plain. This huge cannon was cast at Ahmadnagar in bell metal and is the largest piece of medieval brass ordinance in the world – 15 feet long, 40 tons in weight with a bore of 2′ 4′′, from which an iron ball weighing over a ton could be fired. Above the touchhole is inscribed 'The work of Muhammad Bin Husain Rumi'; a later inscription marks Bijapur's capture by the Sunni Moghul Aurangzeb, 'Defender of the Faith'. Behind the Burj-i-Sherza, within the town, is Haidar Burj, with exterior spiral stairs mounting to a sweeping view over the western approaches; one of its guns is called Lamcharri, Far Flier. The southern Landa Kasab bastion near the Fateh Gate also has a particularly fine cannon.

The reign of the new Sultan, Ismail, saw the Raichur *doab* successfully reclaimed from Vijayanagar, the capital moved to Bijapur, and much fighting with the other sultanates; but his son, Mallu, proved incompetent and was deposed in 1593 after six months, his brother Ibrahim eventually coming to power and establishing the Sunni faith.

In 1557 Ali Adil Shah succeeded and reverted to the Shi'ite creed. He made alliance with Rama Raya of Vijayanagar in order to invade Ahamadnagar, but the fearsome vengeance wreaked by the Hindus there so disgusted Ali that he was very ready later to join Ahmadnagar, and, with Bidar and Golconda, to smash Vijayanagar, which was accomplished at Talikota in 1565. To mark the event, Ali began work on Bijapur's Jami Masjid, an imposing, spacious creation of bays and domes, arches and piers, and arcaded clerestory; it could hold 5000 people. The pavement beneath the great dome is marked by black lines into squares to imitate the *musallah*, prayer carpet, of the faithful; it is said that Aurangzeb ordered this done after he had removed the mosque's rich velvet carpets for his own use. As well as reinforcing the defences, Ali also built within the Arh Qila or citadel, the Gagan Mahal, Heavenly or Sky Palace, that served as a *durbar* hall. It has magnificent arches and a roof gallery for the court ladies.

Ali had married into the Ahmadnagar family to strengthen their alliance, but from the Sultan of Bidar, in recompense for aid against Golconda and Berar, he demanded two eunuchs; one of them murdered him in 1580. His nephew, Ibrahim II, came to the throne, proving able and just, and under his 46-year rule Bijapur returned to the glory of its earlier days. Not only the Muslim and Hindu religions flourished; Ibrahim II permitted Christianity to be practised, and preached, in his lands, even endowing several Catholic churches with land and revenues. He built the Anand Mahal, Palace of Delight, in the *zenana* and the Jal Mandir, a beautiful water pavilion within the citadel.

Situated on open plains, Bijapur has no natural stronghold and the Arh Qila citadel near the centre of the city once stood inside formidable double walls and moat. The city's main gates were all doubled, clad in iron, studded with elephant spikes and defended by twin bastions, with barbicans that would force invaders to make a 90° turn between the two sets of doors. The citadel gate was particularly strong; Hindu piers in the guardroom indicate that at least some temples were quarried by the Muslims for defence restoration works.

There are more than 50 mosques and at least 20 important tombs in and around Bijapur. Some of the other most notable mosques within the citadel are the Old Mosque, converted from a Jain temple; the miniature Makka or Mecca Masjid, a beautiful building made for the court ladies; the Bukhara Masjid; and the delicate mosque and tomb of Mirza Sandal, a noted stonemason. Between the Jami Masjid and the

Malik-i-Maidan, 'Lord of the Battle Plain', is one of the largest cannon ever cast.

Arched bridge to the Athar Mahal.

ABOVE AND RIGHT *The entrance to Taj Baori, the city's main water tank.*

Ibrahim Rauza, tomb of Sultan Ibrahim II Adil Shah.

Jami Masjid.

OPPOSITE *The entrance pavilion to Mihtari Masjid, and below, Gol Gumbad, tomb of Muhammad Adil Shah.*

citadel stand the wondrously decorated Mihtari Mahal gateway and Mihtari Masjid: small but graceful, the latter is 'one of those gems of the builder's art which the Indian's mind at times found such delight in producing'.

Inside the Mecca Gate is the tank Taj Baori, named after the favourite wife of Ibrahim II, and reached by two flights of steps passing beneath a great archway. Outside the same gate is the Ibrahim Rauza, the mausoleum of Ibrahim II, the Taj Sultana and several others of his family. It once stood in a fountained garden and still is very beautiful today. The ceiling is carved with lines of the Quran and flowers, originally gilded against the deep blue background, carvings of a remarkable dexterity and imagination. The windows, too, consist of *jali*-work of Arabic sentences, the spaces between letters letting in the light. It is a marvellous building in every respect, structural as well as ornamental.

The death of Ibrahim II in 1626 coincided with the intensification of the Moghuls' efforts to annexe the Deccan. Diplomacy had kept them at bay thus far but as governor of the Deccan for his father the Emperor Shahjahan, Aurangzeb came close to achieving his aim with Bijapur and Golconda. However, both sultanates were spared for a time by the Moghuls' struggles with the Marathas. In 1665 Emperor Aurangzeb's general, Jai Singh of Amber, defeated the Maratha chieftain Shivaji at Purandar, and prepared to besiege Bijapur. Failing, he was recalled. Muhammad, Ali II and Sikander were the last Sultans of Bijapur. During the minority of Sikander the Abyssinian regent, Khavass Khan, in an attempt to stave off Aurangzeb, offered to marry the child-Sultan's only sister, the adored Padishah Bibi, into the imperial family and eventually the next regent succeeded, against popular opinion, in doing so. But Bijapur was besieged in any case for 18 months, the Deccanis making desperate horseback hit-and-run sorties while they could. Eventually, each side severely depleted by starvation and with only 2000 defenders left, the fort surrendered. Sikander was pensioned off to Daulatabad, where he died 15 years later.

Muhammad Shah had succeeded in 1626 and began work, among other things, on his own mausoleum, simply called Gol Gumbaz or Round Dome, unquestionably one of the most impressive buildings in India. Its great hall is the largest domed space in the world, and the dome itself, dated 1659, is greater than anything in Constantinople, greater than Rome's Pantheon, greater than St Paul's in London, second only, by 15 feet, to the dome of St Peter's in Rome. It is a marvel of construction, the beautiful interior intersecting arches counteracting the vast outward thrust of the dome. There are four seven-storeyed corner towers, each opening onto a remarkable whispering gallery inside the dome: the softest whisper can be clearly heard across the huge intervening space.

After the Moghul ruination, the later Maratha and British rulers of Bijapur undertook some timely restoration, recognising the value of the Adil Shahi legacy. An inscription on the Ibrahim Rauza fairly proclaims: 'Heaven stood astonished at the elevation of this building, and it might be said, when its head rose from the earth, that another heaven was erected. The garden of Paradise has borrowed its beauty from this garden, and every column here is graceful as the cyprus tree in the garden of purity.'

239

VIJAYANAGAR

A ruined bridge over the Tungabhadra river at the metropolis fort of Vijayanagar.

Temple procession avenues of Hampi Bazaar (left) and Achyuta Raya's Temple (right).

Plan of Vijayanagar:
a. King's Palace (with Throne Platform)
b. Mint
c. Danaik's Enclosure
d. Hazara Rama Temple
e. *Zenana* (with Lotus Mahal)
f. Elephant Stables
g. Achyuta Raya's Temple
h. Sulai Bazaar
i. King's Balance
j. Pampatati Temple and Hampi Bazaar
k. Krishna Temple
l. Vitthala Temple

242

All who visited the immense fortified metropolis of Hindu Vijayanagar in its 15th-century heyday were overwhelmed by what they found. Italians, Persians, Portuguese and Russians, none of them strangers to greatness or to opulence, believed it to be the richest city in all India, perhaps in all the East, on a par in size and art and architecture with Rome: a religious centre as well as a magnet for trade in pearls and coral, elephants and horses, camphor, pepper, sandalwood and musk, dealing through its seaports with far-off lands like China, Burma, Malaya, Persia, Africa and Portugal. Today it stands an awe-inspiring ruin.

The site had been occupied since time immemorial – it is identified with Kishkinda, scene of some of the great stories of the *Ramayana*. Properly defended it was, despite its vastness, held to be impregnable: the largest area, including an inner walled citadel and palace, was enclosed by semi-circular lines of walls and ramparts, 60 miles of them, against the hilly south bank of the river Tungabhadra; the north bank was the fortified region of Anagundi. What clataclysmic defeat could have wrought so much havoc?

In 1336 two brothers, Harihara and Bukka, the sons of Sangama, laid the foundations of the kingdom. They had a few years earlier been taken prisoner to Delhi by the armies of the Tughluqi Sultan after the defeat of Warangal, had converted to Islam and gained the trust of the administration. Faced in 1336 with rebellion by the east-coast Hindus, the Sultan appointed the brothers to retake the region in his name. This they did, until continuing dissension in the sultanate persuaded them

Krishna Deva Raya's Throne Platform from where the king watched the Dasara (Mahanavami) Festival, an event represented in bas-relief on its walls.

instead to declare these domains their own. Their reversion to Hinduism was reinforced by the declaration from a religious leader that Harihara, who first took the crown of Hastinavati, or Hampi, was divinely authorised, a god-king of the local deity, Virupaksha. Bukka succeeded in 1354 and immediately began work on a new capital, Vijayanagar, City of Victory.

The rival Hindu kingdom of Hoysala had already fallen to his brother and Bukka increasingly fought with the Bahmani kings; the Sangama dynasty from then on was almost constantly at war with neighbouring kingdoms, Muslim or Hindu, their territory alternately contracting and expanding. In 1447, in the reign of Mallikarjuna, Vijayanagar was attacked simultaneously by the Bahmani Ala-ud-din II and by Kapilesvara, the Hindu king of Orissa. The defence of the kingdom had been largely in the hands of Saluva Narasimha of Chandragiri, and by 1485 he had seized power and managed to stay any further disintegration. His infant son was usurped soon after his own death by the regent and a new dynasty, the Tuluvas, led by Narasa Nayaka, took control in 1490, in time to wage war against the newly formed sultanate of Bijapur under the Adil Shahis. A prime cause for battle between them was the Raichur *doab*, a rich alluvial plain between the Tungabhadra and the river Krishna. Narsing Raya, as he was known, extended his conquests into Drauveda, the Tamil lands, and built forts at Chandragiri and Vellore. One of his sons, Krishna Deva Raya, succeeded in 1509 and became over the next 20 years Vijayanagar's greatest military leader and monarch.

Elephant Stables.

Lotus Mahal in the zenana *compound.*

Vitthala Temple.

LEFT *The main temple pavilion with fine 'musical' pillars, each with a different 'tone'.*

BELOW *A full-scale stone replica of a temple car drawn by a pair of elephants.*

RIGHT *Leogriph carvings and bas-relief figures in the Kalyana Mandapa, Great Hall. Each pillar is carved out of a single block of granite.*

Under Krishna Deva Raya the kingdom of Vijayanagar reached its peak of power and sophistication. His half-brother, Achyuta Raya, lacked all his qualities and lost both land and prestige, failing to control the intrigues of Rama Raya, son of Krishna Deva Raya's minister. On the death in 1542 of Achyuta and that of his infant son, Rama Raya seized power in the name of Krishna Deva Raya's own young son, Sadasiva, forcibly replacing the earlier Brahmani administration with his own adherents. He successfully allied himself with first one Deccani ruler then another in order to make joint attacks on Bijapur, then Ahmadnagar. Such chicanery and the savage treatment by the Hindus of conquered Muslims decided the Deccani Sultans to form a confederacy to crush Rama Raya's overweening power, and in 1565 the battle of Talikota took place. The Hindus were completely routed on the death of Rama Raya; they fled the field and fled Vijayanagar on their elephants, with countless treasures, leaving their glorious city open to robber tribes and to the vengeful Muslims:

Coloured powder used in puja, *prayer ceremonies, being sold outside the Pampapati Temple.*

The main court and gopuram *of the Pampapati Temple.*

'No retreat, no flight was possible except to a few, for the pack-oxen and carts had almost all followed the forces to the war, and they had not returned . . . for a space of five months Vijayanagar knew no rest. The enemy had come to destroy, and they carried out their object relentlessly . . . Never perhaps in the history of the world has such havoc been wrought, and wrought so suddenly, on so splendid a city; teeming with a wealthy and industrious population in the full plenitude of prosperity one day, and on the next seized, pillaged, and reduced to ruins, amid scenes of savage massacre and horrors beggaring description.'

Of the fortifications little survives, but remarkably, over the ten-square-mile site, there are still some buildings left to give an impression of Vijayanagar's former splendour.

The heart of the palace complex was the Hall of Audience and the Singhasan, the Throne Platform, built by Krishna Deva Raya in 1513 to celebrate victory over Orissa. The terraces of these remain to demonstrate their grand proportions and the outer walls of the platform are carved in relief with elephants, dancing girls, camels and scenes from the *Ramayana*. Krishna Deva Raya's court was rich with silk hangings, silver furnishings and exquisite gems, fragrant with the smoke of incense, filled with gifted Sanskrit and Telegu poets and philosophers, dazzling in its sculpture and ornamentation.

Several temples in Dravidian or Tamil style are quite well preserved, like the Vitthala Temple with nearby a life-size stone replica of a *ratha*, a processional temple car; the exquisite Hazara Rama Temple; and two temples dedicated to Ganesha, with enormous granite slabs as roofing. There are everywhere the ruins of once fine, colonnaded bazarrs and among them an arch identified as the 'King's Balance' where the ruler was weighed in gold coins for distribution on auspicious occasions; some early Jain remains; and temples dedicated to Vishnu, the principal deity here after the advent of the Saluva dynasty: a huge incarnation of him, the Narsingh *avatar*, a colossal lion-headed man, looms beneath a canopy to overwhelm the visitor.

There are temples to Shiva, too, like the Pampapati Temple, one of the oldest here and still in daily use, with a huge Nandi bull opposite. Where a temple could not be added to, further enclosures were made round the original shrine, with multi-storeyed gateways or *gopurams*, and sumptuous, many-coloured pavilions, many here with typically exuberant carving on the pillars.

There are several elegant towers in the *zenana*, from which the ladies could watch the festivals and court life. The pretty, arcaded Lotus Mahal is well preserved; its small, screened upper windows suggest a Hawa Mahal, Breeze Palace. There were ranges of guardrooms nearby, for a female guard as well as eunuchs, and outside the *zenana* is a splendid arcaded building, the Elephant Stables.

After 1565 Rama Raya's brother, Tirumala, and Sadasiva took refuge at Penugonda until Tirumala usurped the crown to form the Karnata dynasty, which dwindled in importance except as patrons of the arts, moving again in 1585 to Chandragiri and fading from the scene. Vijayanagar, however, reduced as it is, retains an aura of greatness that can never be eclipsed.

A very rare triple-headed Nandi, the bull of Shiva.

VELLORE

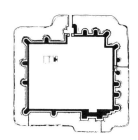

A fort without an army,
A temple without a god,
Women without beauty
And jasmine without scent.

Despite this unflattering description, Vellore is one of the finest examples of military architecture in south India. It is a perfect specimen of a *jala durg*, water fort. Rectangular, with a small projection towards the gate, it conforms to the principles of the ancient Hindu *shastras*, including a moat infested with crocodiles; low causeways over this could be flooded by the defenders. Its double, blue granite walls carved with Hindu reliefs have a broad walk between the

lower, outer wall, and the inner one. Machicolations and bastions project from both levels, and there is a strong bastion before the main entrance across the single drawbridge to the south-east.

Vellore was built towards the end of the 14th century by the Hindu Vijayanagar kings and held by them until their defeat in 1565. A self-styled Raja of Vellore had, on the fall of Vijayanagar, taken control of what had become an important provincial capital, but increased trade rivalry between the Portuguese and the Dutch on the Coromandel coast at the beginning of the 17th century stirred up territorial manoeuvres among the rulers, and Vellore finally fell to the Muslim Adil Shahis of Bijapur.

In 1677, when Shivaji, the great Maratha chieftain, began his campaigns in the Deccan to gain a foothold in the Karnatic, he did so by investing Vellore, by previous agreement with Bijapur's main rival, Golconda. Occupying the neighbouring hills of Sajara and Gajara, the Maratha army successfully blockaded the fort and Shivaji's general, Narhari Rudra, took it after prolonged siege and bombardment.

A present-day devotee worships ancient deities in the fort's Jalakantesvara Temple.

Monolithic pillars carved with gods on horses in the temple's Hall of Learning.

Because of their strategic importance, the Marathas later fortified both these hills, falling back on Vellore when they lost Gingee to Aurangzeb's forces in 1698, but losing Vellore too.

In the 18th century the fort played its part in the turbulent history of the Karnatic, plagued by rivals for the title of Nawab backed variously by the Marathas, the French and the British East India Company. French power in India came to an end with the surrender of Pondicherry to the British in 1761; exactly two days earlier the Maratha confederacy had been decisively defeated and set back by the Moghuls at Panipat. The British took Vellore in 1768, successfully defending it in 1782 against Haidar Ali of Seringapatam, who foresaw its importance in his struggles with the British, situated as it was, commanding the road to his state of Mysore. It was to this fort that the family and retinue of Tipu Sultan were brought by the British after their victory at Seringapatam in 1799, and it was here that a small *sepoy* mutiny took place against the British in 1806.

In that year, the 1500 *sepoys* of the British garrison of the 69th Regiment at Vellore mutinied, provoked by some ill-advised orders from the Commander-in-Chief at Madras concerning the prohibition of beards and caste marks. The officers were shot and nearly 200 British other ranks killed or wounded where they had been imprisoned in their barracks – about half the British force. Some escaped to the ramparts where, under the command of two young army surgeons, they put up a stiff resistance till relief came from a cantonment 14 miles away. About half the *sepoys* were killed or taken prisoner. After the mutiny, Tipu Sultan's family were removed to Calcutta, but their tombs are at Vellore, to the west of the fort. In the old cemetery near the fort entrance is a sarcophagus inscribed to the dead of the 69th.

The most impressive building within the fort is the Jalakantesvara Temple, dedicated to Shiva; remarkably it was almost undamaged during the Muslim tenure of Vellore. There is a beautiful Nandi bull in the courtyard, the gateway of which bears a seven-storeyed *gopuram* of blue granite, with a figure of Parvati dancing on either side. The principal pavilions are important examples of late Vijayanagar style, the pillars in particular being exquisitely carved with different beasts and monsters and gods on horseback.

There are certainly gods in the temple today: like the rest of the fort it is part of everyday life at Vellore. The British built a bridge over the moat and most of the buildings now in use within the fort walls. They cleared and refilled the moat, which today is used for fishing and swimming, the broad walk between the fort walls acting as a promenade and in one place as a tennis court. In spite of the heat at Vellore, intensified by radiation from the neighbouring hills, it has long been known as a health spa; perhaps now it deserves a different proverb.

GINGEE

Gingee was the most famous *giri durg* in the Karnatic; over five centuries every power in the land in turn sought to take it and to hold it, recognising its strategic significance and formidable defences.

The fort is built on three hills forming a triangle – Krishnagiri, Chandragiri and the 800-foot Rajagiri at the apex, which houses the fort proper, Raigarh. An outer curtain wall surrounds all three hills, culminating in the walls protecting the high, usable ground on Chandragiri and Krishnagiri. The citadel's outer bailey, partially moated, was entered by a huge triple gate, with a barbican and heavily guarded courts that would force attackers through six right-angled turns, twice as many as most other forts. Two further gates lead in and out of the inner bailey, and just below the summit the rock is divided by a deep chasm where a drawbridge adjoins a final, narrow gate which just a handful of men could defend against great numbers. From below, the sheer rock face of Rajagiri looks impregnable, indeed unattainable, but a tough two-hour climb through seven gates brings one to the very top.

The powers that ruled from here can be traced in the buildings that remain. Gingee is an ancient fort, founded by the Cholas, a bastion of Tamil culture from the 9th to the 13th century; they strongly fortified the citadel in the latter stages of their era. The Cholas' traditional enemies were the Pandyas of Madura, and by 1442 Vijay Ranga Nyaka, the Pandya Governor of Tanjore, was in control and began the incorporation of the two neighbouring hills, walling them into the present triangular complex. The Governors and their independent descendants held Gingee for over 200 years, and made most of the remarkable temples and palace buildings here.

On Rajagiri itself, one of the most impressive of these is the Kalyana Mahal, a typically Hindu square court with a large, stone-built tank, surrounded by rooms for the Governor's entourage and with a central tower pavilion, with pillared arcade, seven storeys high. A sophisticated water system, using three tanks and two springs, brought water up as far as the sixth floor. Beyond the palace are a stabling block; a vaulted granary – possibly a Maratha addition; a large elephant tank; and the 18th-century Saad-Atulla Khan Mosque, with Persian inscriptions. Saad-Atulla marched against Tef Singh or Desingh in 1714 on behalf of the Nawab of the Karnatic: just north of the Chettikulan pond stands the platform where Raja Desingh's body was said to have been cremated and where his young queen committed *suttee*.

The magnificent 16th-century Venkataramana Temple is the largest temple in the fort, with Tamil inscriptions, a brick *gopuram* or towered gateway, and finely carved granite pillars in the Halls of Learning. Several of these pillars were removed by the French to their settlement at Pondicherry after their occupation of Gingee in the mid-18th century.

The highest citadel of Gingee Fort at 800 feet: the impregnable crown of Rajagiri.

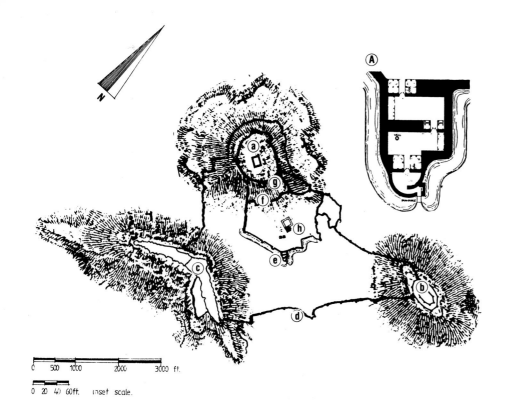

Plan of Gingee:
a. Rajagiri citadel
b. Krishnagiri
c. Chandragiri
d. Outer Gate
e. Triple Gate to inner fort
   (and inset A)
f. Third Gate
g. Triple Gate to Citadel
h. Kalyana Mahal

Krishnagiri and outer fortifications.

256

One exceptional natural feature of the fort was pressed into service by its commanders: poised on a rock stands a great boulder about 20 feet high, with a hollow formed in the centre; this was the Prisoners' Well, down which the condemned were dropped and left to die of starvation.

Krishnagiri is reached by a steep ascent of granite steps all the way up to the top. This fort has two large granaries, wells for *ghee* and oil, an audience hall, a temple with beautiful pillars, and a later Moghul pavilion at the highest point.

After the collapse of the Vijayanagar kingdom in 1665 Gingee fell to the Bijapur Sultanate; but in 1677 the Maratha chieftain, Shivaji, having entered into an alliance with Bijapur's rival, Golconda, stormed into Gingee and it remained a Maratha stronghold until 1698. Shivaji's

A view of Rajagiri and Chandragiri seen from Krishnagiri, all three of which protect Raigarh at their centre.

Krishnagiri citadel with a temple, an
audience hall and large granaries.

successor, Shambhuji, had in 1689 been captured and executed by the Emperor Aurangzeb, who then went on to take the Maratha capital of Raigad. Raja Ram, the new leader, escaped and made Gingee the head-quarters for the Maratha guerillas. Two years later the inexorable Aurangzeb ordered the siege of Gingee under his best general, Zulfiqar Khan, a siege which lasted seven years. The Moghuls failed to cut the defenders' communications and all through the siege the Maratha light horse attacked the besiegers' grain supply and twice ran off sizeable imperial horselines. The demoralised Moghuls, themselves almost in a state of siege and beset by rumours of the Emperor's death, were at the point of withdrawing when a serious rift among the Marathas gave them the chance they needed. In 1698 Gingee became a Moghul possession – though Raja Ram escaped their clutches a second time – and it remained their southern capital until the 1730s, when the centre was moved to Arcot. Gingee later played an important part in the

258

Outer bailey defences guarding Raigarh.

British-French battles to establish who should be the Nawab of the Karnatic: in 1750 the French commander, Bussy, took the fort in a night attack; then in 1761 after a five-week siege, Gingee became the last French fort in the south to fall to the British in the Seven Years' War.

For the local people, the fort is part of their everyday world of rugged hills and vivid green paddy fields: the women move gracefully through the landscape, balancing brass waterpots; the men thresh grain outside the Vellore Gate in the traditional manner, their horses wheeling everlastingly. Gingee has only rarely been visited or photographed by outsiders and a whole day is scarcely enough to scale the citadels and wander among the fortress buildings, to see and absorb all there is to be discovered. A love of beautiful scenery, a passion for hill climbing, an appreciation of historic palaces and temples and of military strategy — any of these, or all four, should bring visitors to Gingee in a state of high expectation.

And there they stand, as stands a lofty mind,
Worn, but unstooping to the baser crowd;
All tenantless, save to the crannying wind,
Or holding dark communion with the cloud.

*Crows now inhabit the honeycombed
shell of the seven-storeyed tower of
the Kalyana Mahal.*

261

'The Rock Fort of Trichinopoly', an aquatint by Thomas Daniell.

The Lalitankura rock-cut temple with its beautiful relief depicting the Ganges flowing from the hair of Lord Shiva.

The rock fort seen from the tank and (right) a panorama across the fort and the town.

The great and venerated rock of Tiruchi rises sheer from the plains to a height of some 250 feet, and from the temple pavilion on top of it, for 20 to 30 miles in all directions there is a fine panoramic view to distant ranges of hills. Inscriptions found on the rock date its known history to the 3rd century BC, and the town was known to Ptolemy, the 2nd-century Alexandrian geographer. Little of the early fortifications now remain: even the 16th-century ramparts and moat have been overwhelmed by houses and the most significant survival is the Main Guard Gate, one of the town's landmarks.

On the Karnatic coast there were three fortified European settlements – Negapatam under the Dutch, Pondicherry belonging to the French, and the British at Madras – and it was in this theatre that the question of mastery over south India was decided, between Dupleix, Bussy and Lally, and Clive, Eyre Coote and Stringer Lawrence. An inscription let into the parapet of a bridge over the Cavery river at nearby Sri Rangam, commemorating Lawrence's defence of Tiruchirapalli and two other actions in 1753, declared that they 'mainly contributed to lay the foundations of the British Empire in India'.

A key to control of south India, the Tiruchi fort was a base for the southern Hindu kingdoms; after the wreck of Vijayanagar in 1565 one of the most important of these was Madura under the Nayaks, who held Tiruchi for a time. It fell at different periods to the Marathas and the Muslims, including the rival Nawabs of the Karnatic and their supporters, the British and the French. There were a number of engagements between the British and the French in this area in the 1750s, the French under Lally being defeated by Eyre Coote in the decisive battle of Wandiwash in 1760. The rulers of Seringapatam both attempted to win Tiruchi from the British in 1780 and 1790, and both failed.

264

The most important remains in Tiruchi today are the temples. Those within the fort are reached by very steep stone steps leading up into the rock from the south. There are stone elephants to be seen, friezes carved with animals and pillars with capitals depicting the lion of the south. The first flight of steps opens out at the level of the main 11th-century defence line onto a street, and nearby is an excavated temple full of superb relief sculpture probably dating from Pandya times. A second flight leads to a very early temple and nearer the summit is the celebrated Lalitankura rock-cut temple, with reliefs that are renowned as masterpieces. More steps ascend to the crowning *mandapa*.

The green island of Sri Rangam and the *gopurams* of its two temples stand out in the view from the top, and should be visited. The Great Temple of Raghunathaswami, the largest in India, dating probably from the 10th century and dedicated to Vishnu, is enclosed by a vast outer wall, sheltering gardens as well as the seven temple courts: the outer one contains a bazaar. All the *gopurams*, at least one of them well over 100 feet high, are brightly painted, and in the court round the central enclosure is the remarkable Hall of a Thousand Pillars, all supporting pediments with plantain brackets; some of the pillars are marvellously carved from one block as men on rearing horses. The Temple of Jambukeswar, dedicated to Shiva, is much smaller, with five courts, but is probably even older than the Great Temple.

After the British occupation, Tiruchi settled down to the quiet life of a cantonment but is notable for the continuance of its religious life, many Churches having founded colleges and missions here since the 1760s. It has been a source of inspiration for pilgrims and for countless artists over many centuries, constantly renewing and enriching its links with the past.

SERINGAPATAM

'The light of Islam and the faith left the world: Tipu became a martyr for the faith of Muhammad: The sword was lost and the son of Haidar fell a noble martyr.'

So reads the inscription on the tomb of Tipu Sultan, whose final defeat at Seringapatam in 1799 gave the British the state of Mysore and complete ascendancy from sea to sea in southern India.

On the breakup of the Hindu Vijayanagar kingdom in 1565, most of the Deccan had been divided between Bijapur and Golconda. Then, in the redistributed balance of power between the last Moghul and first Nizam or Moghul viceroy, and the Marathas, the Hindus re-emerged in strength in the state of Mysore. By 1765, when the Anglo-French disputes had left the British East India Company as a fourth power in the equation, Haidar Ali, a determined and courageous soldier in the service of the Hindu king, replaced that monarch and made Mysore a Muslim sultanate, consolidating his strength and domains against the Marathas and the Nizam until by 1780 he was the Company's main opponent.

The defeat of Tipu Sultan by Lord Wellesley at Seringapatam in 1799.

266

The threat he posed had made strange if temporary allies of the British, the Marathas and the Nizam. However, Haidar Ali successfully bought off the Marathas, the Nizam suffered a change of heart, and Mysore fought vigorously against the British, taking Mangalore, coming to within a few miles of Madras and forcing the Company to come to terms, and even to enter a defence pact with him in 1769. In 1771 when the Marathas attacked Haidar Ali, the British, instead of lending aid as promised, took Mahe, a small French settlement in Mysore state. The Marathas were bought off again by Haidar Ali and in 1780 he took the offensive, initially getting the better of the Company's troops and taking Arcot; then, in 1781, he was defeated at Port Novo. He died the following year and his son, Tipu Sultan, pursued a strong course against the British till in 1784 they entered a second treaty with Mysore.

Neither side set much store by this accord, each determined on supremacy in the Deccan; but the British under Lord Cornwallis in Madras found themselves in a dilemma. Tipu Sultan had taken the Nizam's Bhaghagar, later Hyderabad, this holding being ratified by the British 1784 treaty. However, the Company had already in 1768 promised to hand over Bhaghagar to the Nizam should they ever possess it, and had supplied troops to the Nizam on the understanding that these should not be used against them or their allies – among whom Mysore was not then counted. When the Nizam pressed his claim six years later, the British chose to honour the 1768 treaty, thus as good as declaring Mysore their enemy.

Tipu precipitated war by attacking Travancore in 1789, outclassing the British forces until the end of 1790, when Lord Cornwallis took command. Then the British captured Bangalore and came in 1791 to within a few miles of Seringapatam, but had to withdraw at the onset of the monsoon. They reached the city's outer walls the following year: half Tipu's kingdom was divided between the British, the Marathas and the Nizam, two of his sons were taken hostage, and he was forced to pay an indemnity of £3 million.

Struggles between the Nizam and the Marathas continued. Tipu sought the help of the French as allies, with whom since 1793 the British had been at war. France also had its sights on the East: as Lord Wellesley set out for India, Bonaparte was building his forces for Egypt. Wellesley effectively neutralised both the Marathas and the Nizam and launched two forces at Tipu, from Madras and from Bombay. Refusing all terms, Tipu was killed when his island fort in the Cavery river was stormed in May 1799 and the Mysore throne, for reasons of British policy, was restored to a child prince of the former Hindu Wadiya dynasty.

Close by the spot where Tipu Sultan fell is an attractive walled court-yard with reliefs of serpents beneath banyan trees; it leads to the Water Gate. Tipu's summer palace, the Darya Daulat Bagh, is just outside the east side of the fort, a confection of red and white vertically striped walls in a peaceful garden. Its wall paintings, depicting Colonel Baillie's defeat at the hands of Haidar Ali, were restored by Wellesley and later repainted on the orders of Lord Dalhousie. He also gave the double doors, rosewood inlaid with ivory, for the mausoleum of Haidar Ali and Tipu Sultan, which stands in the Lalbagh further east. The memorial of Colonel Baillie, who died a prisoner, is nearby.

Tipu's Tiger. (By courtesy of the Board of Trustees of the Victoria & Albert Museum.)

Tipu Sultan's tomb.

267

THE MARINE FORTS

Janjira, an island fort in the Arabian Sea.

Think of India and one thinks of the vast, seething interior, peoples of the plains, peoples of the hill country, great events, great cities, amid a mighty landscape. And yet the coastal forts of Maharashtra, land of the turbulent Maratha clans, played a significant role in the later history of India: like ports everywhere, they were entrepots for ideas and cultures but in addition their harbours were the natural object for the vessels of all eastward-trading nations – Arabs, Africans, Dutch, Portuguese, French, British – and battles for possession of them were inevitable.

Janjira was the strongest marine fort in all India, built by Abyssinians in 1511 on an island south of Alibagh below Portuguese Bombay. The leader of the Abyssinians, probably their best sea-captain, was called

the Sidhi and the Abyssinians were collectively called by that name. They came as slave-traders to the Deccan and dealt with the Adil Shahis of Bijapur. In return for this concession they provided armed escorts for the pilgrim ships bound for Mecca out of Janjira, Goa, Surat and Dabhod: corsairs – Dutch or English or from Malabar – were a constant danger to merchant shipping, looting, killing and raping on the high seas from the African coast to the East Indies.

The Maratha chieftain, Shivaji, first attacked Janjira during his campaigns in the Konkan area in 1659. His son Shambhuji in 1682 attempted to tunnel to the island but with signal lack of success. Each time the Marathas assaulted the fort the Sidhi fleet and the Moghul ships from Surat combined to bombard them from the region. Though they tried hard neither the Marathas, nor the Moghuls, nor Portuguese, nor British could ever capture Janjira by force.

The British East India Company had been granted a *firman* by the Emperor Jehangir to trade out of Surat after they had decisively beaten the Portuguese there and at Bombay in the early 17th century. During the Moghul-Maratha struggles, however, the British withdrew from their factories or trading stations at Surat and retreated to Bombay, seizing as they went large numbers of Moghul ships as 'compensation' for their losses on the eastern coast in fighting against the Moghul viceroy of Bengal. It was the Sidhi fleet of Janjira who humbled the British in Bombay, forcing them to pay an indemnity and release the captive vessels in return for the safe discharge of their own people left in Surat.

Janjira protects the city of Murud, one of the ports where Muslims embarked for Mecca. Its Muslim name was Jazire Meharuba, Moon Fort.

OPPOSITE *Bastions with rusted cannons glimpsed through the embrasures.*

270

Janjira lies some way offshore but it is possible to hire a square-rigged *dhow* to visit it. The *dhows* ply from the port of Murud, a tiny place that has hardly moved on from the 16th century: life revolves round the masjid steps and the quayside; women are attired in black *purdah* dress, broken only by a slit for the eyes. The sailors are a wily bunch and must be made to understand that a return fare is being paid, otherwise they could well sail off to fish the silvery, early morning sea. The island is uninhabited now and it might easily be days before the same or any other passing *dhow* would venture in to collect stranded foreigners – and the price for doing so could, of course, be high.

With the shore one leaves behind all present-day concerns. Jazire Meharuba, the Moon Fort, beckons, the more beguiling since one may be sure of approaching it in a manner unchanged down the centuries.

Luxuriant in a palace garden grown wild, Janjira must have been an idyllic place: pretty mahals and terrace walks and mosques, all built on a human scale, cooled by the sea breezes – and secure. Some of the

An Islamic inscription set into the fort walls which are jointed with lead to withstand seawater.

The upper carving shows a lion holding four elephants in its claws, one in its mouth and one in its tail, recording six victories.

A dhow *waits at the main gate into the fort.*

OPPOSITE *The jungle reclaims the empty buildings in Surul Khan's Palace.*

great, rusting guns of Janjira still point from their embrasures: Chavari, its muzzle carved like the jaws of some fearsome monster; Kalal Bangadi; and Landa Kasam. This was the Sidhi Surul Khan's palace; one can still patrol and admire his ramparts of blue-black granite, jointed with lead to withstand the pounding of the Arabian Sea. At the steps by the main entrance is a memorial to six battle victories – the lion of Abyssinia holding six elephants captive. It is almost impossible, though, for today's visitor to harbour thoughts of bloody bombardment into dust or a burning death at sea. This is a quiet, seductive spot to leave, with day darkening into night and blue waters turning gold in the sinking sun, the soft slap of wave on wood the only sound.

Northwards up this western coast are nine other marine forts. The closest to Janjira is called Padmadurga, Lotus Fort, as much for its shape as the carvings on its walls. Sometimes called Kansa, it was built in the late 17th century by the Maratha Shivaji, very much aware that to protect his western flank from the Sidhis, the Portuguese and the British, and to provide an escape route should he be hemmed in on land, he needed to maintain a navy and a line of coastal defences.

Korlai, further up the coast, is a lovely hill fort. Originally it belonged to the Adil Shahis of Bijapur, who built the citadel, but the outer walls are Portuguese; they also built the church here. The city-fort of Chaul nearby at the mouth of a creek was taken by the Portuguese from the Moors in 1522 and held by them till 1739, when the Marathas captured it. The once famous city has altogether disappeared and only the ruins of some churches remain.

The southern approaches to Bombay are next marked by Underi, a Sidhi fort, and Khanderi, another stronghold of Shivaji, described by the British as 'the dagger pointed at the heart of Bombay'. Protecting that heart was Fort St George, bastion of the East India Company. Another Maratha fort, Arnala, commanded the coastline north of Bombay and beyond that was Vasi, a Portuguese holding.

Perhaps more than any other thing, the ever-changing flags flying from these very forts would have told an onlooker how India fared during the course of the 17th, 18th and 19th centuries. Despite the epic struggles that took place on land and the changes in events brought about by the advent of artillery, the course of India's history here was dictated by quite a different development, that of what came to be called the East Indiamen. These ships, a combination of merchantman and man-of-war became, with the British tars who sailed them, a byeword for speed and manoeuvrability under sail, their gunners every bit as good as those of the sister navy that in time ruled the waves. First chartered in 1600 by Elizabeth I, the captains of the Company were daring and original men, as indeed they all were, whatever their nationality, who ventured far across these seas.

The Moghul and Maratha ships were smaller, slower and bore fewer guns, conceived more as a coastal navy and in many cases dependent upon oarsmen rather than on sail. Vijaydurg was the main base for the Maratha navy; according to the East Indian Directory it was 'an excellent harbour, the anchorage being landlocked and sheltered from all winds. There is no bar at the entrance, the depths being from five

OPPOSITE *Padmadurga, Lotus Fort, so named both because of its shape and its lotus carvings. Also called Kansa, it was built by Shivaji between 1668 and 1672.*

BELOW *An abandoned cannon still points towards a long-forgotten enemy.*

to seven fathoms; and from three to four fathoms inside at low water.'

The navy had been founded in 1659 and grew in size from 50 to 400 vessels within 20 years – many coastal fishermen, familiar with the tricky winds and currents, were very ready to hazard their lives and fortunes with Shivaji, not just to defend their homelands but, like any fighting sailor, in hopes of prize money. The fort protecting the 'excellent harbour' was built on a rocky headland jutting into the sea. Its walls and 27 bastions are even thicker and sturdier than those of inland forts: at high tide the sea batters at Vijaydurg, the constant enemy.

Between Vijaydurg and the Sidhi Janjira lie four other forts: Kanakdurga and Suvarnadurga, both translatable as Golden Fort, the former a shore fort and the latter a very picturesque island fort only 20 miles from Sidhi territory, with the smaller Gopalgad or Aanjanwel and Bankot-Himmatgad in between. Gopalgad, once an embarkation point for Mecca, is now very dilapidated, and Bankot suffered, too, in the British occupation of 1790, when it was renamed Fort Victoria.

Suvarnadurg was the home base of the renowned Kanhoji Angria who, like his father before him, served the Marathas. He had been born there and had grown up among the Koli sailors, learning their lore, learning their seamanship, but he was made second-in-command of the Maratha navy for his success in a land engagement. Suvarnadurg was attacked by the Sidhis; Kanhoji, captured during a sortie, later managed to escape and successfully took command of the fort's defence. He rose to full command of the Maratha navy in 1698 after the death of Shivaji and patrolled the coast so effectively that the run between Goa and Bombay became a veritable gauntlet for other shipping.

In coastal waters, the smaller Maratha vessels had some advantage over the East Indiamen: they could slip into shallow creeks to avoid the Britishers' heavy guns and if ever the larger vessels were becalmed, the *galbats* and *ghurabs* could be rowed out under cover of darkness towards the stern of the enemy, thus avoiding any danger of a broadside, and discharge their own prow or broadside three- or nine-pounders at close range. Once the British guns were out of action, more *ghurabs* could come up with boarding parties. In this way Kanhoji took the *Otter*, the *Robert* and the *Success* and blew up several other ships, quite enough for the British lion in Bombay to deem him not just a nuisance but a pirate, and to stir forth to bring him down. They found it hard enough, failing, even acting with their Portuguese trading rivals, either to capture Vijaydurg or to blockade it.

The Dutch fared no better, and Kanhoji's son continued to harry the Europeans until the 1750s, when dissension among the Marathas destroyed their independent strength. In 1756 the Angria fleet was wrecked at Vijaydurg by British fire and the Maratha Peshwa entered into an alliance. Devgad; Sindhudurga, the fort built by Shivaji where his statue stands, and re-named Fort Augustus by the British; Terekhol; Fort Aguada in Goa, now a spectacular Taj hotel; and Sadishivgad – in time all these fighting forts were neutralised, and today the village fishing fleets jostle in and out of their palm-grown ports, intent only on capturing the sea's bounty or to visit their neighbours up and down the coast.

THE BRITISH FORTS

The first Fort William at Calcutta was built in 1696, with a clear field of fire over the deep-water anchorage and protected on the landward side by extensive and unhealthy swamps at the delta of the Cooum river. Its foundation came about as a result of the fluctuating goodwill that existed between the British and the Moghuls. In 1664 and 1670 the British had successfully defended Surat, their west-coast factory or trading station on the Gulf of Cambay, against Shivaji, thus earning the approbation of Emperor Aurangzeb in his 30-year struggle to contain the Maratha forces. However, the British in Bengal fell from grace in 1688 when they ignored a request from the Nawab, the Moghul's viceroy or governor, to abstain from fortifying their factory on the Hoogli. This had not been done as an unfriendly act towards the Nawab but towards the French, with whom the British expected war shortly to be declared. Surat was also fortified in defiance

'The Old Fort, the Playhouse and Holwell's Monument, Calcutta 1786–8'. An aquatint by Thomas Daniell.

276

of Aurangzeb, who then promptly expelled all the British from his territories. A later Nawab, Ibrahim Khan, invited the Company, in the person of Job Charnock, to return. Instead of building on the Hoogli, he chose the better anchorage of Calcutta.

After Aurangzeb's death in 1707, the Nawabs gradually increased their dominions to comprise, by 1738, Bengal, Bihar and Orissa, enjoying a fair degree of autonomy and consequently the same degree of conflict with the Marathas as their Moghul overlords. In 1756 the Nawab was the young Siraj-ud-daula, contending not only with the Marathas but domestic attempts to unseat him, Hindu unrest and anxiety about European intentions – the French and the British were again fortifying their factories, this time in anticipation of the Seven Years' War. On 16 June 1756 the armies of Siraj beseiged the British at Calcutta and on 20 June they captured the garrison, most of the civilians having retreated to the safety of their ships. This was the occasion of the notorious Black Hole incident: a reported 146 persons were confined by the Nawab's forces overnight in the local jail, a room 18' by 15' with two small windows. Only 23 people emerged alive the following day, a calamity now generally attributed to negligence rather than considered a condign Nawabi punishment for their resistance. Nevertheless, the outrage felt by the British over the incident was deep-seated and became ingrained: the Black Hole, the Battle of Plassey and the Mutiny were for generations the sum total of most Britons' knowledge of India.

Calcutta was retaken by Clive and Watson in 1757 and six months later the Nawab's forces were defeated at the Battle of Plassey and the Nawab himself was killed. Mir Jafir became Nawab, with Clive's help, and was installed on the 17th-century black stone *musrud* or throne of the Nawabs, now in the *durbar* hall of the Victoria Memorial Hall, along with a collection of the Daniells' paintings, and much else of interest.

The present Fort William was begun in 1758, facing the Maidan or Battle Plain, once much used as a parade ground and a fashionable promenade. The octagonal walled fort was never attacked, though it was well protected by a wide, deep moat that could be filled from the river. The arsenal and the garrison church of St Peter, built in the style of St George's Chapel at Windsor, are well worth a visit. A much earlier place of worship lies more than a mile south of St Paul's Cathedral at the south-east of the Maidan: Kalighat, from which Calcutta takes its name, site of a riverside temple to Kali, consort of Shiva.

Bombay may also have taken its name from a Hindu goddess, Mumbai, a form often given to Parvati, reincarnated wife of Shiva. The Sultan of Gujarat ceded Bombay to the Portuguese in 1534 and the place did not change hands again until the 1660s, when it was ceded by the Portuguese to England as part of Catharine of Braganza's dowry on her marriage to Charles II. The king later made Bombay over to the East India Company for an annual rent of £10, paid until 1730. It was a President of the Company, Gerald Aungier, who began the work of transforming an unhealthy swamp – Bombay then consisted of seven islands at high tide and malodorous mudflats at low tide – into a thriving city.

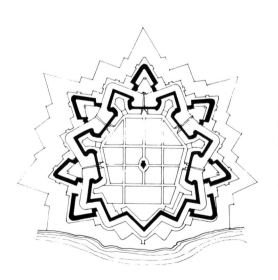

Plan of Fort William.

Bombay Castle and Fort St George commanded the harbour, which was the refitting base for a large part of the British fleets then to be found in Indian waters. The fort was star-shaped with triangular bastions, interposing ditches and earthworks between the main defences, and the lower outlying walls lined with artillery. Very little remains of the fort today, though the castle has survived.

Land to the north of Madras had been given to the Company as early as 1639 by the last of the Vijayanagar line, the Raja of Chandragiri, and a small fort of St George was begun in 1644, lower down in the Cooum river, close by an island. The fort withstood attacks by Aurangzeb, and the Marathas, but fell in 1746 to the French, being restored to the British three years later by treaty. In 1758, the French under Lally once more besieged the British under Colonel Stringer Lawrence, but after two months they withdrew in the face of a newly arrived British fleet. Three times over more than 20 years the independent Sultans of Mysore, Haidar Ali and his son Tipu Sultan, threatened Fort St George before Mysore's eventual defeat in 1799 at Seringapatam.

The garrison church of St Mary, built between 1678 and 1680, was the first English church in India. Like the fort, it was built by Streynsham Master, who was Governor here at that time, and contains many interesting memorials. Some of the Church plate was presented by Elihu Yale, a subsequent Governor, much better known for his later endowment of Yale College in America. The southern gate of the fort is called San Thomé in reference to the tradition that St Thomas was martyred a few miles away at Little Mount; his remains are said to lie

'The British Fort at Bombay'. An 18th-century engraving by Jan van Ryne.

beneath the nearby cathedral of his name. Repainted in yellow ochre, the fort now houses government offices, though cannon still flank the entrance to the officers' mess, today a museum with displays of armoury and uniforms, and a collection of paintings and engravings; the long portrait gallery was once the Assembly Rooms for the garrison and the civilian community.

'As well for the honour of this our realm of England as for the increase of our navigation and for the advancement of our trade.' Thus did Queen Elizabeth I charter the East India Company on 31 December 1600. Two centuries later 'Company Bahadur' governed India in a way never wholly achieved by any of its predecessors.

Inland some way from Fort St George lies Arcot, where Clive made his reputation as a captain by capturing and defending the fort with a small force against great odds in 1751, during the battles for control of the Karnatic. All the Nawab's mosques here have disappeared; only a few pillars of the earlier Shiva temple still stand, carved with cobras, clasped in jungle; while of the British fort only the Delhi Gate remains, bearing an inscription to Clive. The conquerors of Hindusthan have come and gone, and perhaps Kipling's words from *The Naulahka* best judge their transitory possession:

> And the end of the fight is a tombstone white
> With the name of the late deceased,
> And the epitaph drear: 'A Fool lies here
> Who tried to hustle the East.'

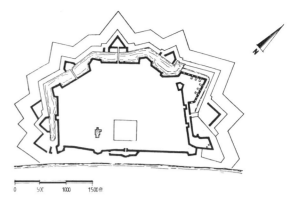

Plan of Fort St George.

'Fort St George, Madras'. An aquatint by Thomas Daniell.

279

THE PHOTOGRAPHER'S

V.F. with bodyguards at Ajaigarh.

The ascent by 'doolie' at Raigad.

Forts and castles have long held a fascination for me. Twenty years ago I toured the Crusader castles from Methoni in Greece to Krak des Chevaliers in Syria. Later, on my many visits to India, everywhere the startling sights of forts on hills filled me with a longing and determination to explore them and to record them in photographs. It took four separate visits, between 1980 and 1985, to achieve my ambition. It was tough, varied and exciting. I enjoyed the challenge and the fun, and feel very privileged to have had the opportunity to experience such unforgettable and unusual adventures.

Part of the appeal was the inaccessability of some of the more remote and rarely visited forts. As I ascended to each new one my spirit soared with a feeling of exhilaration and sheer ecstacy. To photograph Kalinjar and Ajaigarh I had a long and exhausting climb to 800 feet under a relentless sun. But what unexpected rewards awaited me on reaching the summit when I discovered the forts contained magnificent examples of early sculpture. I picked my way between headless torsos and their severed heads lying side by side – carnage in stone. I trod among a wealth of images: a reclining Shiva, a dancing Ganesh, a Nandi bull, a Vishnu boar. I longed for a sack but then thought better of it. Their rightful home is where they fell.

At Talbehat, in a simple hollowed-out log canoe, I risked life, limb and cameras to photograph the fort from the crocodile-infested waters. Hanging precariously out of helicopter windows, I took aerial photographs of Samthar and Patiala. On an elephant I rode up the steep slope to Amber fort and, less successfully, on a camel at Jaisalmer. Four men carried me in a 'doolie' – a basket on poles – up the 1400 steps to Raigad. Overlooking a precipice, it was an anxious journey and, since it had to be undertaken at sundown, it was pitch dark by the time we reached the top where we spent the night at the rest house. My appearance was greeted with utter amazement. Later, the journey down was even more alarming!

At Rajgad I was literally hauled up the final rocky ascent, cameras and all, by my two guides, Appa Dashpande and Professor P. K. Ghanekar. But, for me at least, the stupendous view from the top was well worth the effort. I cannot speak for my guides!

Kumbhalgarh I found totally deserted except for the temple *pujaris*, a few local inhabitants and the stooped old *chokkadar*, who conducted me through the fort, opening up the doors to dusty palace buildings and temples with a heavy bunch of ancient, curiously shaped keys, and spoke with nostalgia of the far-off days. Alone I walked for miles around the wide and imposing ramparts, peering through embrasures from which, until ten years ago, tigers were shot, for this is the true 'Sher Khan' country.

Hazards and the unexpected are part of the fun of India. When I

TALE

inquired of two pundits deep in conversation the most suitable path to a certain fort, I was summarily dismissed with the disdainful reply, 'Madame, we are presently engaged in some very meaningful dialogue.' On the approach to Garhkundar through wild and rocky jungle, one of my armed companions quipped, 'Madame, I hope you can shoot.' 'Yes, if I have to,' I replied, grabbing the rifle a mere second or so before a wild boar charged out of the undergrowth. The accuracy of my shot could only be attributed to sheer terror. On another occasion we arrived at the District Commissioner's rest house in the Banda District of Bundelkhand to be told that dacoits had made off with all the beds the previous day. Dacoits in 1983! I chose to spend the night sleeping on a table in preference to a bedroll on the floor among the rats.

On every horizon in Rajasthan and Bundelkhand one can make out the contours of a fort. There are, literally, hundreds of them all over the countryside. They rise out of the deserts, out of lakes, out of mustard fields, out of rocky jagged hills. They are part of the terrain itself. And although they have blended into day-to-day life and few pay them much attention, every fort has its own distinctive character, its myths, its awesome reputation. For me it was a journey into the mists of time, to the realm of legend and history, of chivalry and valour when the honour of a queen could provoke great battles, and when many victories were hollow because the vanquished chose *johar* rather than suffer at the hands of their conquerors.

As I travelled the length and breadth of Hindusthan, experiencing the variety of its colossal landscape, I began to grasp a faint concept of the country and the people who had been held in its spell. In spite of all its fortresses, its invaders and its defenders were forced one by one to abandon their cause. The land is too vast; sooner or later it will make a mockery of every scheme and race who seek to improve it.

A verse returns constantly to my mind to serve as an ironic reminder:

> India, grim stepmother of a kind:
> If a year of life you lend her,
> If her fortress gates you enter,
> The door is shut – you may never look behind.

This book is a tribute to all those who once lived and died in these historic fortresses; to all those warriors who defended them; to the courageous souls who committed *johar* and *suttee* and whose hands and stones commemorate them in the walls. Impressed on my own memory will always be the occasion when I thoughtlessly left my camera in a fort temple. It was later returned to me by a local woman who said, 'Madame, do not leave this behind – it is your wealth.' That wealth is now offered in this book.

At the summit of Rajgad.

Water transport at Talbehat.

The Maharaja of Jaipur with his daughter, Princess Diya Kumari.

V.F. and Rita Sharma at Deogarh.

This book has been a combined effort by many people who helped contribute along the way to make my fervent ambition become a reality. I should like to acknowledge here all those friends and strangers and send to them my deepest gratitude and thanks.

I shall begin by thanking the Government of India and the State Governments, together with the individual owners of the forts, for granting me permission to photograph.

I very much appreciate the kindness and courtesy shown me by everyone who assisted me in India; my guides, bodyguards, and drivers who escorted me safely throughout the land, often working long hours, and who joined in the spirit of adventure.

My thanks to His Highness, the Maharaja of Jaipur, whose ancestors built the forts of Amber, Jaigarh, Nahargarh and many others. His keen interest in military history and arms is evidenced by the Foreword he has so kindly contributed. My thanks also for all my happy stays at the City Palace, Jaipur, which included the festivals of Holi, Diwali, and Christmas.

My special appreciation and thanks to Tikki and Jutta Oberoi, loyal friends over the last fifteen years, who were deeply interested in my work right from the start and were a tremendous encouragement on all my Indian 'camera ventures'. Sadly, when Tikki died in 1984 I lost a dear friend and supporter, but to my great joy Jutta rose to the occasion and co-financed the production of this book in memory of her husband.

My thanks to the Sharmas for writing the historical content of the text, a difficult task when so much of the unrecorded history is passed down only by local repute whispered in the bazaars and under the village peppel tree, where legends are mixed up with the local folklore. Rita and Vijay were a delight. First introduced to me by the Maharaja of Samthar, we became instant friends and companions, bonded by our common desire to produce this book. Rita, chatty, smiling and informative; Vijay, always in command but with a sense of humour which breaks through his shy exterior as the sun disperses the morning mist. They accompanied me to all the Bundelkhandi forts in a cavalcade of jeeps and armed personnel.

My gratitude to Christopher Tadgell for his invaluable contribution to the architectural content of this book and for his diagrams of many of the forts, which give a clearer insight into their military structure and significance. Together with his own photographs of Gaur, his hard work and dedication to the project are substantial.

My very special thanks to my wonderful friend and co-ordinator in Delhi, Rena Ripjit Singh, on whose floor we spread out the maps and late into the night planned together my many complicated trips throughout the length and breadth of the land.

My thanks also to Inder Sharma, Chairman of Sita Travel, whom I originally met in 1969 on my first trip to India, whose personal interest and assistance has helped the book to materialise; and to my old friends, Camelia Panjabi and Nasib Chand Katoch of the Taj Group, for their advice and generous hospitality.

It was the greatest help having Chryssie Lytton Cobbold with me on my trips to the southern and central Indian forts. Herself an excellent writer and photographer, she was a wonderful fellow traveller of endless ingenuity, especially at Janjira where we risked being stranded forever. The men in the *dhow* who had taken us across to this island fort refused to wait and prepared to set sail, until Chryssie waved some rupees from a parapet and saved the day.

I am grateful to my sister, Serena, for agreeing to drag an entire Serenissima group, which included my mother, all the way to Mandu in order to take some extra photographs for me.

To my supporters at home: Robin Birkenhead, Monny Curzon and Jeremy Saunders, whose encouragement and sense of humour gave me the confidence to continue, along with sundry gurus and pundits – my heartfelt thanks.

My appreciation to the Hobhouse Gallery for allowing me to reproduce the aquatint of the Red Fort at Delhi, and the Thomas Daniells prints of the Rock Fort at Tiruchirapalli, the Bridge at Srinagar and the British forts at Calcutta and Madras.

My thanks to Ronald Clark who designed the book at my publishers, Collins, and whose patience, kindness and endurance were unflagging over the many hours and weeks; to Gill Gibbins, who had the complicated task of editing and putting together the text of the book, the historical content, the architectural content and my descriptions of each fort.

Finally, a very special thankyou to Ranjit, His Highness the Maharaja of Samthar, who arranged my trips throughout Bundelkhand and introduced me to life in his fort where all the old traditions are still observed, where no one except the Royal Family has the privilege of sleeping in a bed and where meals really are moveable feasts that arrive at a different court, roof, or pavilion every day. A carpet was simply laid down and, sitting crosslegged, we ate at low silver tables. When we went for a ride the entire inhabitants of the fort, 200 strong, followed us for the first half-mile, and at every village shots were fired in greeting. But the best was yet to come. After our long day riding I asked if I might have a bath 'English style' instead of the customary bucket of water, and to my relief was shown a magnificent large copper bath complete with brass taps from which hot and cold water gushed at the turn. I sank thankfully into this luxurious tub and was wallowing like a buffalo, head back, when suddenly I became aware of two beady eyes looking down on me through holes in the ceiling. With a shriek I leapt from the bath and lunged for the nearest towel.

With great indignation I told the story to Ranjit when I joined him for dinner. Far from offering an apology, he enthusiastically explained that as there is no hot and cold running water in the fort, a man is sent up to the roof with buckets – and when he sees the taps being turned on he obligingly pours the hot and cold water down the pipes! It could only happen in India.

I hope that all who read this book will get as much pleasure from it as we have had in producing it, and that enthusiastic travellers will go and see for themselves these monuments to India's illustrious past.

V.F. 1985.

V.F. and Chryssie Lytton Cobbold at Janjira.

The Maharaja of Samthar with his jaghirdars.

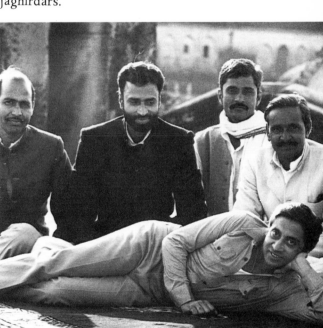

283

GLOSSARY

agni – fire
antepura – inner town
apadanas – multi-columned halls
apasaras – celestial dancing girls
avatar – incarnation

bagh – garden
bailey – outer wall of fort
baldachino – canopy on pillars
bangaldar – bowed or curved roof
bansur – archer
baori – well
baradari – audience hall
baraka – benign influence
bazaar – shopping quarter
bhakti – devotion to a personal god
bhavana – hall
bhisti – water carrier
bidri – damascene metalware
bihat – village
buland darwaza – lofty portal
bund – embankment

caravanserai – inn for caravans
chadya – awning, eave
chahar bagh – four-square garden
  (setting for tomb)
chattri – memorial canopy
chauth – Maratha tax
chenar – plane tree
chokkadar – watchman
chor minar – totem of victory
chota – little
crore – ten million

dacoit – bandit
daulat khana – abode of majesty
dhabdar – armourer
dhak – tropical tree
dhangar – shepherd caste
dhanva durg – desert fort
dhow – single-masted ship
dipmal – lantern pillar
diwan – hereditary prime minister
Diwan-i-Am – hall of public audience
Diwan-i-Khas – hall of private
  audience
doab – alluvial plain
donjon – castle keep
doolie – basket carried by bearers
durbar – royal court of assembly
durg – fort

fakhir – member of Islamic religious
  order
ferenghi – outsiders
firman – order

gadi – royal throne
gajala – elephant pond
gajvyala – elephant panel
garbla-griha – womb chamber, inner
  sanctum
gauli – cowherd caste
ghat – steps to a bathing place
ghurab – small oared boat
giri durg – hill fort
Gita – Hindu holy book
gole – massed formation of lancers
gopi – milkmaids of Krishna
gopuram – temple gatehouse
gur – sugar cane

hamman – bath
harem (haram sara) – women's
  quarters in Muslim dwelling
Hathi Pol – elephant gate
haveli – merchant's house
Hawa Mahal – breeze chamber
hindola – swing

jaghir – grant/liege holding
jaghirdar – liegeman
jala durg – water fort
jali – shutters
Jami Masjid – Friday mosque
jar – decay
jehad – holy war
jharokha – place of appearance
jizya – tax on Hindus
johar – voluntary immolation of
  women and children

kal – death
kamangar – bowyer
kara – iron bangle
karindar – feudal retainer
kauri – crushed shell
kesh – unshorn hair
khanqah – retreat
Khas Mahal – exclusive pavilion in
  palace
kirpan – small steel dagger
kuchcha – short breeches

kunbi – cultivator caste
kund – tank
kungha – hair comb

lakh – one hundred thousand
lingam – phallic emblem of Shiva
liwan – vaulted space

madrasah – college
mahal – palace
mahi durg – mud fort
maidan – field open to defenders'
  fire
maithuna – loving couple
mandapa – pavilion for attendants
  or ritual performers
mandir – Hindu or Jain temple
mansabdar – holders of high
  command
Marusthali – Land of the Dead
masjid – mosque
merlon – raised crenellation
mihrab – recession in *qibla* wall
mimbar – pulpit
minar/minaret – tower for calling to
  prayer
misl – martial brotherhood
moti – pearl
motte – mound or keep of castle
murti – images of gods and goddesses
musallah – prayer carpet
musrud – throne of Nawabs of
  Bengal

Nagina Masjid – jewel mosque
nakkara – huge kettledrum
Nandi – bull of Shiva
Nandi Mandapa – temple pavilion
  for Shiva's bull
nara durg – fort on a plain, protected
  mainly by men

pachisi – form of backgammon
padma – lotus
pakhar – armour for an elephant's
  trunk
pancharanga – flag of the Rathores
panhari – water carrier
panj-hazari – commander of 5000
paur – gate
pietra dura – hard stone inlay

284

pol – gate
prakara – wall enclosing temple compound
prasada – walled complex of courts and pavilions
puja – prayer ceremonies
pujari – priest
pundit – learned teacher
pur – strengthened earthwork
purdah – seclusion or screen to prevent women being seen by strangers

qibla – axis of Mecca or direction of prayer

Raja Bhavana – hall of public audience
Rang Mahal – pleasure palace

ratha – processional temple car
rawala – women's enclosure in temple

samadhi – cenotaph, cremation monument
sandeshmukhi – ruler's perquisites
sarkar – administrative district
sawan bhadar – water tower
sepoy – Indian soldier serving British
serdab – subterranean room
shakti – motivating force of deity
shastra – treatise
shikar – hunting
shikara – spire
Shish Mahal – palace of mirrors
Sikh – disciple
sikligar – swordsmith
squinch – arch below a dome

sufi – holy man
Suryavanshi – descendant of the sun
suttee – widow's suicide on husband's pyre
swarajya – homeland

tal – lake
talao – tank
talar – columned portico or pavilion
tika – anointing
tilak – Hindu forehead mark
tonga – light two-wheeled vehicle
torana – gateway

vana durg/vriksha – forest fort
vimana – walled complex of courts and pavilions

zenana – women's enclosed quarters

INDEX